CREAM
Strange Brew

Chris Welch

Published by Castle Communications Plc
Book Division, A29 Barwell Business Park
Leatherhead Road, Chessington, Surrey KT9 2NY

Copyright © 1994 Castle Communications Plc

Design: Brian Burrows
Paintings/Illustrations: Brian Burrows

Photographs supplied by: Pictorial Press Ltd,
London Features International Ltd, Rex Features,
Retna Pictures, Redferns

ISBN : 1 898141 80 0

1

CREAM
Strange Brew

CONTENTS

Chapter One
PROLOGUE

A group of brownies scampered around the church hall raising clouds of dust, while a caretaker grumbled and banged doors. The message was clear. It was time for the strangely-clad trio of long-haired musicians who had invaded their territory to stop disturbing the peace of a suburban afternoon with their incomprehensible thunder.

The new band's first rehearsal was drawing to a close and the hall would soon be handed back to the young girl scouts for their games and rites, but not before a music reporter clutching an inky notebook had reassured a worried-looking manager: 'The band sounds great!'

The group relaxed and clustered around a partially-erected drum kit set up to one side of the dimly lit hall, joking and smoking. They had just finished playing the three numbers that were the only items in their repertoire. It seemed a casual, almost careless start to the career of a group that would achieve astonishing success, transform the popular music scene and would one day be elected into the Rock And Roll Hall Of Fame.

The band was Cream and I was the privileged eye-witness. Having invented the phrase 'supergroup' especially for the new team of Eric Clapton, Jack Bruce and Ginger Baker, it was a proud moment. Their manager, Robert Stigwood, looked reassured, and the band were happy, and eagerly anticipating an exciting future.

Strange to think, as we left the hall in a North London suburb that sunny June afternoon in 1966, we were all nearly wiped out only moments after the band had begun!

THE LEGACY

Cream was a proud title. It suited a band made up of the most exciting players to emerge from the melting pot of the British R&B scene that thrived, amidst a wave of crusading zeal, at the height of the Swinging Sixties. It came about as a result of the need to alleviate the frustrations of star sidemen, who felt restricted working with lesser musicians. Baker, Bruce and Clapton needed to PLAY and Cream would give them the ultimate musical freedom. It gave a lot more. It encouraged them to write, experiment, explore different directions and, ultimately, it gave them huge financial and artistic success.

But there was a price to pay. Cream also became a demanding machine that ate up their strength, resolve and creative spark. When Cream turned sour, the trio broke up exhausted, just as they had reached a peak of popularity. Their career had lasted just two and a half frantic years.

During their time together, from June 1966 to November 1968, Cream virtually created the concept of modern rock music, based on improvisation, original songs and driving guitar, bass and drums. The Who and The Kinks pioneered power chords and heavy riffs, but it was Cream that unlocked the pent-up energy of a new wave of high energy musicians. They paved the way for such bands as the Jimi Hendrix Experience, Led Zeppelin and even The Mahavishnu Orchestra. Their brand of heavy rock, with its strong instrumental and vocal attack, would also provide the blueprint for heavy metal, and a whole generation of hard rock and blues bands.

When they started, they had no clear cut idea of what they were trying to achieve, beyond the fact they knew they could be successful. They had virtually no material, and had to create songs that eventually became hailed as classics in spare moments during a hectic touring schedule. In the climate of the times, they were expected to work within the parameters of pop music, while their own roots were in jazz and blues. To add to the confusion, their personalities and backgrounds were vastly different and this led them on a permanent collision course which tore them apart.

Paradoxically, there was a lot of love between them. When the band was at its happiest, they were united by the desire to make music and succeed. Although Cream left a searing mark on Eric Clapton in particular, and its memory would haunt the rest of them for evermore, it wasn't always the bitter and fraught experience some claimed.

Cream was a fulfilling, dynamic if short-lived phenomenon. They soared across the rock firmament like shooting stars, and refused to succumb to the temptation of over-staying their welcome like so many bands who later became branded as 'dinosaurs'.

They made only four albums, and after a series of club dates hardly ever played in their home country. Most of their live work was devoted to heavy tours of America where audiences, mostly unfamiliar with Cream's predecessors from the British club scene, were stunned by their power, expertise and cohesion. When they broke-up, newly-won British fans, who had been waiting to see them, felt cheated, even betrayed. Yet such was the warmth of their reception that when Cream played their farewell concert at London's Royal Albert Hall in 1968, the band wondered whether they had, after all, made a mistake. But it was too alter the course of history.

In their heyday Cream enjoyed hit singles and mega-selling albums. Songs like 'I Feel Free', 'Strange Brew', 'Sunshine Of Your Love' and 'White Room' achieved international chart success and have since become rock standards. Their albums 'Fresh Cream', 'Disraeli Gears', 'Wheels Of Fire' and 'Goodbye' sold in millions. As a 'live' concert attraction, they quickly outgrew the clubs and pubs that were home to most British blues groups, and conquered the world's most prestigious venues. When they played at Madison Square Garden, in New York City on November 2, 1968 they were awarded a platinum record for the double LP 'Wheels Of Fire', which had achieved $2 million worth of sales.

Critics raved about the band's daring fusion of rock, blues and elements of jazz, and praised the virtuosity of Clapton, Baker and Bruce. They were accorded the accolade of a BBC TV documentary Omnibus, produced by Cream fan and critic Tony Palmer, who later went on to become one of the country's top film directors. His film of their last Albert Hall concert has become a best selling video, reviving cherished memories and introducing new generations to their music.

During the height of the psychedelic era they were adored by hippies from San Francisco to London's Kings Road. Clapton especially was idolised as a trendsetter, who set new fashions in dress and hairstyles. When Eric appeared with an Afro hairdo, or a sported a military tunic, eager fans became look-alikes when they flocked to Cream's concerts.

More significantly, other musicians wanted to emulate the brilliance of Clapton's guitar work. Jack Bruce set new standards for bass guitar players and was hailed as one of the most powerful singers in rock. Ginger Baker helped liberate drumming with a dynamic, free-wheeling style that inspired a whole new generation of players.

Amidst all the praise, they had their share of criticism and detractors. At best the band could deliver imaginative picaresque songs, and interweave them with aggressive, exciting improvisation. Sometimes they lapsed into over-long solos, relied on repetition and when the creative spark failed to ignite, stood accused of going through the motions. One reviewer referred to their 'empty virtuosity'. They were capable of lapses of taste and were sometimes misguided in their choice of material. They would freely admit this in interviews, and Clapton himself went through a period of decrying Cream's work.

In hindsight, given more time and tighter direction, Cream could have achieved the cohesive strength and consistency that Led Zeppelin subsequently attained, but Cream were the pioneers, exploring new territory. They were essentially a band of their time, responding to external influences as best they could. They played what they knew and the world had cause to be grateful for their existence. Cream suffered from all the torments of the Sixties; idolisation, pressures of fame and crises of identity – conditions not always helped by drugs, money worries and the stress of life on the road. They also endured their own unique form of inner tension and competition: the need to play at full pitch every night went beyond being a pleasure and was in danger of becoming a nightmare.

Cream was never just a happy bunch of ex-school friends out for a laugh, as was the case with so many British and American bands who later found themselves blessed with good fortune. They were an elite task force of professionals and had to deliver what the public wanted. But nobody held a gun to their heads. Ultimately, they were masters of their own destiny. They lived and worked hard, and achieved much of lasting musical value. The saga of Cream was a cause for celebration, not recrimination.

Years after their demise, rare film footage surfaced of the band rehearsing at London's long-forgotten Revolution club. Shot by a French film crew, it showed Baker, Bruce and Clapton tearing into an intensely powerful version of 'Spoonful'.

Speaking of the newly-discovered footage, their old colleague and songwriter Pete Brown said: "The nice thing about that was that you could see how happy they were together. That's how I like to remember them."

In 1993 the trio enjoyed an emotional reunion, when they played together in public for the first time in 25 years at the Rock'n'Roll Hall Of Fame Induction Ceremony. A lot had happened to them all in the intervening decades, and they had undoubtedly grown older and wiser. However their personalities might have changed, their playing skills had, if anything, improved with age and they locked back together in a kind of musical bear hug. It proved it hadn't all been a dream – they really were The Cream.

Chapter Two
RHYTHM & BOOZE

A heavy black Bakelite telephone on a battered wooden desk at my office in Fleet Street rang with a peremptory clamour. It was late on 'News Day' – the few hours allowed each week to concentrate on filling the news pages of the world's hippest music paper. I had been a reporter on Melody Maker since 1964, flung into the maelstrom of the Swinging Sixties, Beatle Mania, Mersey Beat, and the Pop Boom. Some thought the MM was a 'jazz paper', and it was true that the staff were composed of 100 per cent jazz and blues fans, but the MM had always reflected all shades of popular music from its inception way back in 1926.

Throughout the Fifties and well into the Sixties, the MM had been 'The Bible Of The Profession' supporting the British dance band scene, perhaps with greater enthusiasm than it covered American jazz. But the circulation was often in a parlous state, and a rather sniffy attitude towards the onset of rock'n'roll didn't help. Their upstart rival, the New Musical Express, would dominate with its enthusiastic coverage of chart-oriented pop and rock.

The problem of a direction for the MM was solved by the Trad Boom, spearheaded by a new wave of highly professional traditional jazz bands that achieved unprecedented success in the early Sixties. The Three Bs, Chris Barber, Kenny Ball and Acker Bilk provided a ceaseless flow of front page stories and interviews, as the men in bowler hats, armed with clarinets, trombones and banjos gained hit records and national fame. A bigger revolution was around the corner. Overnight, The Beatles' cries of "Yeah, yeah, yeah" swept aside the sounds of 'Stranger On The Floor' as Acker Bilk's greatest hit was derisively known. As the pop revolution spearheaded by Liverpool's finest gathered momentum, so the music press adapted to changing times. The MM radically changed its layout, abandoned the old dance bands to their fate (even to the extent of throwing away a priceless heritage of historic photographs), and devised an abrasive, tabloid approach to the new pop journalism. The work of avuncular Scots editor Jack Hutton and his dynamic, relentless assistant Ray Coleman they propelled the paper into a new era of success.

It was only just in time. On the day I arrived as a raw recruit, I was assured by dissidents within the ranks that the paper was about to close and that the whole pop scene was dying. I responded to this grim news by getting drunk in the local pub and being violently sick in Fleet Street.

I was convinced on that first evening that I would not last a week on the paper, perhaps not one further day. But the next day was 'press day'. The soothsayers of doom were at the printers, and some very nice PR people from the record companies were asking if I would like to interview the Yardbirds, the Rolling Stones, Burt Bacharach, Dusty Springfield, The Beatles... I stayed.

Despite the upheaval at the MM, (still described by some bitter jazz fans years and years later as an 'act of betrayal'), there was still a strong feeling among the staff that the best of pop music could be given the same respect accorded to jazz. The Beatles had swiftly earned that respect on a global scale and set a precedent that would last for decades. It benefited the MM in many ways to approach the new generation of pop musicians with a reasonably serious, more in-depth approach.

In the days before tape recorders, stories and interviews had to be kept relatively short. But there was no doubt that the great bands of the time still regarded it as an accolade to be featured in the MM. Most pop stars had grown bored with the routine of interviews. Taking a serious interest in their music helped break down the barriers and establish a rapport... then you could ask them what they had for breakfast.

And so during the first two of 16 subsequent years on the MM I had been able to enthuse about all the great upcoming musicians who were creating such exciting music in the clubs, as well as chronicle the daily adventures of the chart stars of the day. After a hard day chatting up Sandie Shaw about the perils of singing in bare feet, or taking Sonny & Cher shopping for clothes in Carnaby Street, I could drive my black Ford Consul to such clubs as The Flamingo, The Marquee, The 100 Club, Scotch Of St. James and The Cromwellian to listen to Eric Burdon & The Animals, Georgie Fame's Blue Flames, The Spencer Davis Group, Chris Farlowe & The Thunderbirds, Brian Auger's Trinity, Rod Stewart's Steam Packet, Zoot Money's Big Roll Band... and The Graham Bond Organisation.

BAKER'S IDEA

But getting back to that phone call in June 1966... the growling, chuckling voice on the line from darkest Neasden wanted to tell me about a great new band being put together. The caller was Peter 'Ginger' Baker, the drummer from the aforementioned Graham Bond Organisation. The new band would feature himself, together with his old bass playing partner Jack Bruce and... get this... Eric Clapton! And who was going to manage this extraordinary new outfit? "Old Stigboot!" It should have been front page news – but the cover was already done. Instead the story went inside in a few terse paragraphs. It was enough to cause a sensation among those thousands of fans who went every week to see the extraordinary roster of R&B bands of all styles who packed the clubs in those pre-disco days. Eric, Jack and Ginger were already heroes as far as they were concerned. The idea of them coming together in an all-star band was almost too much to take.

It certainly caused a shockwave among the managers and band leaders who thought they had first call on these musicians' services. Within hours of the MM hitting the streets, I was inundated with phone calls demanding retractions and press releases issuing denials. I learned that day that the more vehement the denial, the more likely a story was to be true.

The headline on our exclusive story was: 'Eric, Jack & Ginger Team Up' and the piece went on to say:
"A sensational new 'Groups' Group' starring Eric Clapton, Jack Bruce and Ginger Baker is being formed. Top groups will be losing star instrumentalist as a result. Manfred Mann will lose bassist, harmonica player, pianist and singer Jack Bruce; John Mayall will lose brilliant blues guitarist Eric Clapton and Graham Bond's Organisation will lose incredible drummer Ginger Baker. The group say they hope to start playing at clubs, ballrooms and theatres in a month's time. It is expected that they will remain as a trio with Jack as featured vocalist."

Two weeks later the story was confirmed, despite the howls of protest from the managers of Manfred Mann and John Mayall's Bluesbreakers. Robert Stigwood, who had been manager of the Graham Bond Organisation, told me he had signed the new band. "They will be called The Cream and will be represented by me for agency and management. They will record for my Reaction label and go into the studios next week to cut tracks for their first single."

Robert confirmed that the band would make its debut at the National Jazz And Blues Festival at Windsor. In the meantime, Jack Bruce would continue with Manfred Mann and Clapton would stay with John Mayall. Ginger Baker would leave Graham Bond on July 20, 1966, to be replaced by Jon Hiseman.

Just a few months before the story broke, I had come up with an idea for a 'Groups' Group' in an article that proposed an imaginary line-up of players from the best bands of the day. The phrase would later be changed to 'Supergroup' to reflect the commercial success that such a line-up could enjoy, but the original concept was to celebrate musicianship. It was rather like the 'all-star' bands to be found in jazz.

We asked a dozen group musicians to chose their favourites and I put in my own two penn'orth. Among the voters were Mick Jagger, Spencer Davis, Ray Davies, Eric Burdon, Paul Samwell-Smith, Chris Farlowe, Keith Moon, Paul Jones, Tony Hicks (of the Hollies), Steve Marriott, Georgie Fame and Tony Crane (of the Merseys).

Ginger and Jack with Graham Bond and Dick Heckstall-Smith

My votes produced a band that would include Steve Winwood (lead guitar and vocals) and Ginger Baker drums. Although each member of the Cream would get some votes, nobody concocted a line-up with all three. The ultimate Groups' Group, based on the number of votes for each contender, consisted of Eric Clapton (guitar), Bruce Welch (rhythm guitar), John Entwistle (bass), Brian Auger (organ), Ginger Baker (drums) and Steve Winwood (vocals) – actually closer to Blind Faith than Cream.

The three men who would eventually achieve lasting international fame in The Cream had all enjoyed varying degrees of success and recognition during their formative years.

I'd first met Eric Clapton when he was a shy young mod in The Yardbirds, and I'd got to know Jack Bruce after I'd first seen him pounding a double bass in Bruce Turner's Jump Band at a jazz festival.

Eric was already a star with a devoted following and many of the best interviews with him in the early days were by my colleague on the MM 18-year-old Nick Jones.

Between us, we were in the unique and exciting position of covering the rise of a wave of young musicians who would make history. Naturally, it wasn't always easy to convince the older and more sceptical about the importance of these new players, and Nick finally quit the MM in angry frustration. But he kept me on my toes and was often quicker to respond to the buzz on the street. It was Nick who assured me that Clapton was being revered as 'God' by his fans, and was being accorded an unprecedented level of hero worship on his gigs with the Bluesbreakers. I managed to tear myself away from Georgie Fame & The Blue Flames at the Flamingo to go and see Eric with the Bluesbreakers at a gig in Putney. It was no exaggeration to say that everyone at the gig was in awe of the moustachioed figure whose guitar playing seemed blessed by an almost mystical power.

We were all impressed by Eric, but such was his command over audiences that he hardly needed any further introduction. Or so it seemed. Taking Eric at face value as a highly-rated lead guitarist who seemed self-contained and assured meant that ultimately many failed to fully understand the inner conflicts and musical ambitions that motivated him. Eric was always one step ahead of everyone around him. Change and movement meant more to him than being conveniently slotted into a safe, rigid category.

However, there was one member of Cream who I had championed since I first heard about him from musicians like Graham Bond and Charlie Watts. The Stones' drummer had consistently praised Ginger Baker, who had replaced him in Alexis Korner's Blues Incorporated, while Bond proudly boasted that Ginger was 'the greatest drummer in Europe', adding the European rider as a courtesy to the great American drummers. Ginger had other ideas. He was pretty sure that aside from his idols Max Roach, Art Blakey and Phil Seamen, he was the greatest drummer in the world.

Bond had first raved to me about Baker when the former was still a bebop alto sax player on the modern scene. So I knew of the drummer's reputation long before I joined the MM and it was a priority of mine to win him recognition.

I was just blown away by the sheer dynamic attack Ginger brought to the drums. His was a unique style, incredibly daring in its day. He broke all the rules that inhibited most British jazz and pop players. His blitzkrieg approach, involving a spectacular assault on the tom toms and bass drum, was violent, unorthodox, unpredictable and tremendously exciting.

But despite his reputation as a hell-raiser, both on and off the kit, he was a conscientious band player, who had been raised in both traditional and modern jazz environments. He took such matters as drum rudiments and time-keeping very seriously. His 'take no prisoners' approach was anathema to sections of the jazz establishment, but he found freedom and fulfilment in the Graham Bond Organisation, where jazz, blues and rock were mixed with a very un-British confidence and bravado.

THE TIME BOMB

Ginger could be, as he confessed at our first meeting, "a bit of a monster". But despite his reputation for being difficult, bad tempered and cantankerous, I always found Ginger to be warm, generous and surprisingly soft-hearted. As a tough, seasoned and cynical musician who could upset and even frighten people with a glare, he only reserved his contempt for those he thought were going to rip him off or prove treacherous. With his fiery temperament and Irish ancestry, Ginger could be a ticking time bomb – or a warm friend. What he most valued was respect for his musicianship and personal loyalty.

Baker was born in Lewisham, South London on August 19, 1939. He grew up in neighbouring New Eltham on the borders of Sidcup and went to school in Woolwich. As a teenager he was filled with a restless energy which he employed training and competing as a racing cyclist. This undoubtedly gave him the strong leg muscles which later helped him play double bass drums with such speed. However, his first instrument was the trumpet, which he played in the local Air Training Corp band. Their drummer also played with a trad jazz band led by Dick Charlesworth, and Ginger became intrigued by the idea of playing drums himself. The two lads would get out all the ATC band's military drums for fun and hammer away on them together.

Baker was also keenly interested in modern art and modern jazz, and with his flaming red hair and penchant for wearing bright green suits, he quickly became known as a rebellious beatnik. From his earliest days, despite his wild, eccentric appearance and his artistic flair, Ginger was a business-like achiever, determined to try his hand at anything. In later years he would become involved in sculpture, painting, rally driving and polo.

29

Ginger had always nurtured plans to become a professional racing cyclist... until he bought his first drum kit at the age of 15. "I was a cyclist and I wrecked my bike!" recalls Ginger. "I had been into drums from a listening point of view for quite a time. I used to bang on the table with knives and forks and drive everybody mad. I used to get the kids at school dancing by banging rhythms on the school desk! They kept on at me to sit in with this band. The band wasn't very keen, but in the end I sat in and played the bollocks off their drummer. And that was the first time I'd sat on a kit. I heard one of the band turn round and say: 'Christ, we've got a drummer' and I thought, 'Hello, this is something I can do'."

"I had been into drums from a listening point of view for quite a time. I used to bang on the table with knives and forks and drive everybody mad. I used to get the kids at school dancing by banging rhythms on the school desk"

He described his first kit as "a bit alarming". It was a flimsy toy set which he bought for three pounds. He had wanted a kit that would have cost twelve pounds but he'd already spent seventy on his racing bike and his parents couldn't afford to give him any more. He finally raised the money by getting a job in commercial art working for sign writers and later in an advertising studio. Ginger formed a band which included his cousin on banjo and a couple of friends on trumpet and trombone.

Then he saw an advertisement in Melody Maker. The Storyville Jazz Men, a local trad jazz band led by Bob Wallis, needed someone to beef up their rhythm section. He played a gig with them and, despite the fact that he'd only been playing a few months, got the job. At the age of 16, Baker left home, quit his day job and spent a year on the road with the band.

He acquired a more professional second-hand drum kit and built up a good reputation. He even recorded with top clarinettist Acker Bilk, and was then asked to play with Terry Lightfoot, who ran one of the big name bands of the day.

"Then I got fed up with my kit," recalls Ginger. "I got this great idea for using Perspex. It was like wood to work on, but it was smooth, and it would save painting the inside of the drum shell with gloss paint. So I bent the shells and shaped them over a gas stove..." Ginger laughs at the memory of his crude experiments. "I cut them all out and pieced them together with proper drum fittings. I made it in 1961 and used it up until 1966 when I got my first Ludwig kit."

Ginger says he used the home-made kit on the first two classic Graham Bond LPs, 'The Sound Of '65' (for which I wrote the sleeve notes), and 'There's A Bond Between Us'.

Right from the start Ginger got his own sound and style and I remember watching fascinated along with the rest of the audience when I first saw him play with Alexis Korner at one of the early National Jazz & Blues festivals. He was intense, passionate and played as if every beat was torn from his body. If he missed a beat or dropped a stick, the audience felt his pain and frustration, and when he reached a crescendo and a whirling epic drum solo took off, everyone shared his personal joy. If he had played the saxophone or guitar, it would doubtless have been the same experience – a battle of mind over matter. "The way I play – I know now, more than ever – is something I was born with," Baker told me. "The whole approach, the way you hit the drum, is achieved by listening to the sounds you make. I could always play. When I joined the Storyville Jazz Band I told them I'd been playing for three years. In fact I had only been playing three months."

Ginger listened avidly to early New Orleans jazz drummers like Baby Dodds who played with Louis Armstrong. "I fell in love with what he was playing. Baby Dodds was the link between western military drum techniques and African drummers. He was the man who first successfully married the two. He was the first jazz drummer."

Ginger also listened to Alton Red who drummed with Kid Ory, and Zutty Singleton, before he discovered be-bop and modern jazz. As he absorbed the records of Charlie Parker and Dizzy Gillespie he heard the fluid, inventive rhythmic backing of drummer Max Roach. "He was the Guv'nor. But when I started playing, trad jazz was the thing, and it was the easiest thing to play and the best music to start off with as a young drummer.

But things started to go awry when I started to play Max Roach style. As soon as this happened, Terry Lightfoot nearly swallowed his clarinet. He'd say: 'I want four to the bar on the bass drum, nothing else!' So I told him to get lost."

Ginger's vigorous defence of his stylistic freedom meant he was out of a job. He'd only been with the band for six months but ended up having a row with all of them.

In 1959, he went off with guitarist Diz Disley on a three month stint in Copenhagen, then went on a Scandinavian tour with gospel singer Sister Rosetta Tharpe. Back in England he returned home to live with his parents and found that the house next door was empty. It proved a useful hideaway where he could make as much noise as he liked. Even so, the racket coming through the walls drove his mother mad.

"The whole approach, the way you hit the drum, is achieved by listening to the sounds you make. I could always play. When I joined the Storyville Jazz Band I told them I'd been playing for three years. In fact I had only been playing three months."

He was determined to study and practised drum rudiments for nine hours a day. He went to London's West End and hung out in Archer Street, then a famous meeting place for musicians looking for work. He wanted to be a professional musician, but under pressure from his parents he got a temporary job in a factory, loading trucks.

Eventually he got another band job. "I got a reading gig, and I couldn't read. I had to learn to read music in a fortnight, to get the gig. It took me a week to find out what a repeat sign meant. I couldn't figure out why I was getting to the end of a part and the band was still playing!"

By sheer perseverance Baker mastered the mysteries of arrangements and written parts sufficiently to get by and he was good enough to be able to fake the rest.

He moved to Cricklewood in North London and within three months he met and married Liz, a charming and patient lady, who would see Ginger through the tumultuous years that lay ahead.

With the help of friends he got a job playing with Irish dance bands at the Galtimore ballroom. One of the bands played swing in the style of Stan Kenton and Shorty Rogers as well as Irish music. He studied harmony and wrote an arrangement of 'Surrey With The Fringe On Top'.

It was a corny enough piece, but it gave Ginger a great deal of satisfaction to hear a band playing his work. He played at the ballroom for nearly a year, and fitted in gigs at American air bases and a trip to Germany. His big goal in life was to break into the tight knit modern jazz community, and he eventually freelanced at Ronnie Scott's Club. "I was rather controversial," recalls Ginger. "I was always 'too loud!' But I don't like these guys that play like a metronome. I know I'm a bit of a monster. I have always been big-headed, but people whose playing I liked always liked mine, and that kept me going."

Ginger joined the Johnny Burch Octet, which he still believes is one of the best groups he ever played with. He also played with the Bert Courtley band and worked at all-night sessions at Soho's Flamingo Club. He almost landed a top job with the John Dankworth Orchestra, but many of the band had misgivings about employing such a temperamental player. Gradually he found himself frozen out of London's modern jazz circuit. It wasn't just to do with Baker's legendary temper. His passionate approach to drumming was considered too disturbing.

"In those days I played like a madman and got emotionally involved in the music. Some people don't like that. They feel they are losing control of the band. A lot of drummers just played what they heard on record. I was always playing myself. I had influences, obviously, but when I was playing modern jazz I was always accused of being a rock'n'roller because I need to lay down an off-beat. But then, so did Art Blakey. They didn't like this loud drummer playing off-beats, and getting the audience clapping their hands, and dancing about. That was most uncalled for. You were supposed to sit up and listen and drink your drink. But I never considered myself a rock'n'roller, I was always a jazzer."

The music scene was about to undergo a sea change. Big bands and trad and modern jazz groups faced a new challenge from rhythm & blues. British musicians and fans had for years supported the revival of many aspects of American music. The whole post-war traditional jazz movement (called Dixieland in the States), had rested on the enthusiasm of a few revivalists dedicated to recreating the authentic sound of New Orleans jazz. Now there were new discoveries to be made. Chicago-style electric blues pioneered by artists like Muddy Waters, Howlin' Wolf, John Lee Hooker, Chuck Berry and Bo Diddley was rediscovered. All over the country aspiring singers and guitarists, tired of commercial rock'n'roll and disillusioned with elitist jazz, found themselves embarking on a blues crusade. R&B provided a wonderful opportunity to play exciting music that wasn't too complex, and would appeal to a young audience hungry for excitement. When the newly emerged Rolling Stones played in a tent at the 1963 National Jazz & Blues Festival at Richmond, the audience literally ran away from the big stage where Acker Bilk was playing, to seize upon the sensational new sounds of Mick Jagger, Keith Richards, Brian Jones, Charlie Watts and Bill Wyman.

"In those days I played like a madman and got emotionally involved in the music. Some people don't like that. They feel they are losing control of the band. A lot of drummers just played what they heard on record. I was always playing myself."

As a local newspaper reporter, I had the great good fortune to be present at this historic moment. It was on a hot weekend in August when Rhythm & Blues achieved its great British breakthrough. In my review I announced:
"Right from the first appearance by a little known Liverpool group The Mastersounds, it was clear the jazz bands were going to take second place in popularity to the savage beat of the R&B bands. Come Sunday evening, during the last few hours of the festival, a seething mass of fans jammed in a marquee at the rear of the grounds cheered and cheered again Richmond's own Rolling Stones, while Mr Acker Bilk's band plunked dutifully on

the main stage before docile jazz fans seated in neat rows.
"The compere for the show, Bill Carey secretary of the National
Jazz Federation, viewed the swaying masses waiting
impatiently for the Stones to set up their equipment. The
expression on his face changed from delight to amazement, then
bewilderment and worry. 'Shake it up', he kept saying to the
slow handclapping, yelling crowd. 'But look after yourselves. If
anyone climbs on stage we will stop the show. If anybody faints
pass them out over your heads'."

As The Stones, all long hair, pouts and wiggles, tore into 'Come
On' and 'I'm A Hog For Your Baby', trad jazz with its clanking
banjos became a distant memory. Mick Jagger shaking his
tousled mass of hair and a pair of battered maracas had to be a
more exciting spectacle than portly gentlemen studiously
blowing clarinets.

The same day I saw the Cyril Davies All-Stars, Graham Bond
with Ginger Baker, Long John Baldry and Georgie Fame & The
Blue Flames. Everyone present was smitten by the 'new' music
and I wrote:
"It was easy to see why these new groups were so enormously
successful at what was supposed to be a jazz festival. Most of
the jazz offerings were polite, prissy and depressingly
unoriginal. It may have been saddening for jazz fans to see many
of their own number, hard-to-please beatniks, and Richmond's
teenagers, now the first citizens of R&B, deserting the scholarly
gentlemen of jazz in favour of the rebellious barbarians of
rhythm and blues. But for this situation, jazzmen have only
themselves to blame, having deserted the beat for so long. Bill
Carey was shouting at the end of the festival: 'This has been
rhythm & blues and you have made the Rolling Stones the stars
of the festival!'"

Another new star at the festival as far as I was concerned was
drummer Baker. The first impression I had of him was of a red-
haired kid, grinning and pounding away a huge ride cymbal, and
tearing into his big old snare drum as if his life depended on it.
He had become involved in R&B when he joined Alexis Korner's
Blues Incorporated in August 1962, taking over the drum chair
on the recommendation of Charlie Watts. Ginger told me later:
"Charlie Watts is a nice guy and a very good player. Alexis
Korner helped me become a non-monster."

Another musician who liked, helped and understood Baker, was
modern jazz drummer, the late great Phil Seamen. He came to
hear Ginger one night and later they practised together and
talked. Ginger would always pay tribute to Phil as one of the

greatest jazz drummers of all time, and years later, after the success of Cream, he would take active steps to help revive Seamen's career.

"Phil heard me play in the All-Niter Club which used to be the Flamingo on Wardour Street," recalls Ginger. "Tubby Hayes (the sax player) had apparently been in there and heard me and ran over to Ronnie Scott's Club and told Phil to come down and hear me. When I got off stage I was suddenly confronted by my hero."

In February 1963, Ginger left Alexis with Graham Bond and Jack Bruce to form the Graham Bond Organisation. Bond had been with the band for three months when one night they did a gig in Manchester which featured just Bond, Bruce and Baker. They went down a storm and in March 1963 they gave in their notice and quit Alexis to form the new band. Tenor sax man Dick Heckstall-Smith joined six months later and a classic British R&B band was born.

"Charlie Watts is a nice guy and a very good player. Alexis Korner helped me become a non-monster."

Ginger stayed with Bond for three and half years, until 1966 and the formation of Cream. The Bond years were tremendously exciting. Bill Bruford, drummer with Yes, one of the innovative bands of the Seventies, cited the band's instrumental recording of 'Wade In The Water' as crucially important. Apart from the passionate sax and keyboard playing, the rhythm section proved a revelation, with Jack Bruce creating an aggressive new sound on amplified 6-string bass guitar, and Baker attacking his kit with cataclysmic force. The whole piece swung with a fervour unknown in British jazz, and it was probably the first true jazz-rock fusion record.

JACK BRUCE

Jack and Ginger had first got together way back in 1961 when Baker was playing with trumpeter Bert Courtley's band. During a gig in Cambridge, Bruce had asked to sit in. Ginger had been against the idea until he heard how well Jack coped with the changes on a difficult ballad and then tore into a fast 12-bar blues. Although a clash of Scots and Irish temperaments would mar their relationship for years to come, they nevertheless formed a mutual respect on a night which saw their musical destinies inextricably linked.

Jack Bruce was much more than a virtuoso bass player. He was a great singer, with a powerful, soulful style, and blew a mean harmonica. The first time I saw him singing with the Graham Bond Organisation at a loud, poorly-attended gig at London's 100 Club, I wondered why he wasn't the lead vocalist. Graham, whose idea of singing was to bawl himself hoarse, tended to hog the vocal chores, but whenever Jack was allowed to sing, the effect was mesmerising.

He was born John Simon Asher Bruce, on May 14 1943 in Bishopbriggs, Lanarkshire, Scotland.

He had wanted to be a musician from childhood and his parents bought him a piano to encourage him to study music while at school. He left at 16, and at 17 won a scholarship to study cello at the Royal Scottish Academy Of Music in Glasgow.

"When I was a young school boy I always wanted to play the bass, but was put on the cello because I just wasn't big enough to handle the monster," recalls Jack. "At 15, having grown, I realised my first ambition and played bass in the school orchestra. I then went to music college but I didn't stay very long. They didn't dig what I was doing and I didn't particularly think what they were teaching me was going to help me very much. I got quite frustrated at the college, because it was very old fashioned. I was very interested in modern composers like Stravinsky, and the teachers were very old – almost Victorians! A lot of them thought music had died with Richard Strauss. I was also getting into modern jazz and trying to get them to take it seriously was very hard. I liked the MJQ and I thought it was great that they were using classical forms. I'd bring in their records like 'The Golden Striker' and they would just pooh-pooh it."

Jack's mother was the main driving force in encouraging her son to study music. He had started off as a singer in choirs before becoming a boy soprano soloist. He would enter Scottish music festivals and won a few competitions.

"I used to get incredibly nervous, though, and almost throw up beforehand. I still do get stage fright, but as I kid I couldn't handle it. It would be just me and a pianist, and they'd be marking me while singing Schubert. It was very competitive because the same half a dozen kids entered. My mother ensured that I had vocal training, which has stood me in good stead over the years. I knew how to project from the abdomen as opposed to most pop singers who sing from the throat, which is why a lot of them have vocal problems."

*"When I was a young school boy
I always wanted to play the bass,
but was put on the cello because I just
wasn't big enough to handle the monster."*

This ensured Jack's vocal style would be imbued with unusual depth and power.

"It was something people either liked – or didn't like," recalls Bruce. "Frank Zappa liked it very much. But I don't think Eric was much in love with it. He thought in Cream it was the wrong kind of singing for that kind of music, but it's just the way I happen to sing! My feeling is that you bring yourself to the music. You don't have to be anything. There are no rules. The kind of music we became involved in starts with self-expression, so I don't agree with him on that."

When Cream hit the road, Jack was certainly equipped to take on the chores of singing lead, night after night, without fear of losing his voice, but says: "We did suffer, like most bands in those days, from the lack of a decent PA."

After quitting college, Jack went off to Italy to play double bass with a jazz band. He'd already had some experience playing in pit orchestras and his reading ability meant that despite his youth, he could get a gig with virtually any band he liked.

"I used to work in Glasgow in the Palais bands when I was still

at college. In fact that's partly why I left, because you weren't allowed to make a living from playing while you were studying. They had a rule that you weren't allowed to do that. I didn't agree with that because I also liked the money! It was a question of either staying at college or gigging. I was getting great experience playing in jazz clubs and learning Thelonious Monk tunes, which for me was just as important as studying classical harmony. The college didn't agree, so I left."

In 1961 Bruce saw an advert in the Melody Maker placed by the Murray Campbell Big Band in Coventry. He travelled down for an audition at the Mecca Ballroom and played a difficult piece called 'One Bass Hit' recorded by celebrated bassist Ray Brown with the Dizzy Gillespie Orchestra.

"We did suffer, like most bands in those days, from the lack of a decent PA."

"I was fresh from college and sight-read that – immediately. They were blown away and I got the gig. I went to Italy with that band but it became a small band in the style of Louis Prima, playing a shuffle type of rhythm & blues. It was very strange because we were playing variety theatres and the whole band were wearing kilts. Then somebody ran away with all the money and we got stranded in Milan and had to be repatriated. We spent six weeks in Milan with no money and lived on carrot stew!"

Jack returned to Glasgow then finally went to London for the first time. He went to straight to Archer Street. "I went down The Street, and got a gig at an American base – in Italy." Jack was just 17 and the deal was he had to go to France then drive the band to a town near Venice. "I had a driving licence – but only just. I'd lied about my age. And I had to drive this 1940s Mercedes with a trailer on the back carrying a Lowry organ – over the Alps! I'd never really driven before. Anyway, we made it and stayed quite a while on this base."

On his return to the UK, he joined Jim McHarg's Scotsville Jazz Band. "Jim McHarg was the bass player, but he got fired by his own band and I got the band leader's gig! We came in at the tail end of the trad boom. I was never a trad fan, and wanted to get into modern jazz... but at least we didn't have to wear kilts."

BRUCE MEETS BAKER

Jack was playing with the Jim McHarg Band at a May Ball at Cambridge when he first saw Ginger Baker play. "During the interval, when I wasn't playing, I went to the cellar and saw this incredible pick-up group. Dick Heckstall-Smith (tenor) had put it together with Ginger and a bass player who has since died."

Jack was amazed by the sounds the group were getting and the level of free-wheeling improvisation. He saw that if he could sit in, he could prove to himself how good he was on bass. Up until then he had been sacked from all his groups for being too experimental. Dick Heckstall-Smith, doubtless backed up by Ginger, tried to discourage Jack from sitting in, fearing he was just a student who couldn't play or would be unable to cope with their arrangements.

Eventually Jack got on the stand and played well enough to make Dick want to track him down later and get him into Alexis Korner's band.

Jack recalls his first impressions of playing with Ginger Baker: "He looked just like a demon, sitting there with his red hair with the kit of drums he'd made himself. I have never heard drums sound as good as those home-made ones. I'd never heard a drummer like him and I knew that I wanted to play with him."

When Bruce joined Alexis Korner, he and Dick discretely campaigned to get Charlie Watts replaced by Baker.

"It was a great time for me, because I was playing in quite a few different bands. With Alexis we'd play at the Marquee and his club in Ealing. We also did a lot of society things and that was a revelation. I saw how the other half lived. I had come down from Glasgow and found myself playing at Lady Londonderry's Ball. She was the lady who married Georgie Fame and later killed herself. At that time she was the Belle of London. We played this amazing gig with Alexis Korner on guitar, me on bass, Charlie Watts on drums and Benny Goodman – *the* Benny Goodman on clarinet."

"We also played Lord Rothschild's polo parties, attended by the Duke Of Edinburgh. Alexis had all these connections because he was a bit of a 'Hooray' on the quiet. I remember one night when Ginger got really out of it and fell asleep in Lord Rothschild's bed. He didn't mind, but he said something to me, and I got the needle – as I did a lot in those days – and ran down the drive, with Lord Rothschild begging me to come back!"

His Lordship had just brought over an entire team of Argentinian polo players – hence the party. Jack believes this was probably triggered Ginger's subsequent passion for the sport. "That's when it all started. As far as I know he wasn't into horses in Neasden!"

"I remember one night when Ginger got really out of it and fell asleep in Lord Rothschild's bed. He didn't mind, but he said something to me, and I got the needle – as I did a lot in those days – and ran down the drive, with Lord Rothschild begging me to come back."

Bruce and Baker played with Blues Incorporated alongside Alexis and Graham Bond, until their traumatic bust-up. "We were with Alexis for a long time, until Graham resigned – for us. Alexis got really upset. He thought I had left him in the lurch. But it was Graham who handed in mine and Ginger's resignations, without even telling us. It was a real Graham stroke."

However, the Graham Bond Trio was established with Bond featured on alto and organ. "There was a lot more alto than organ," recalls Jack. "He was playing in the style of Ornette Coleman with a lot of free improvising. Graham didn't really concentrate enough on the alto once he got into playing Hammond organ. I was still playing double bass. John McLaughlin came in on guitar for a while, then when he left, Dick Heckstall-Smith came in."

The Graham Bond Organisation was adored by fans, but it was too far ahead of its time to achieve much beyond popularity on the club circuit. Attempts at making pop singles, encouraged by their manager Robert Stigwood, were mostly disastrous, like their dreadful version of 'Tammy' which appeared on their brilliant debut album, 'The Sound Of '65.' They were at their best playing sultry instrumentals like 'Spanish Blues' and a roster of blistering blues tunes such as 'Hoochie Coochie Man', 'Got My Mojo Working' and 'Traintime'. The latter was a tour de force for Jack on harmonica, while 'Oh Baby' gave Ginger Baker a chance to deliver what is still regarded as one of his best drum solos on record.

Although the album was cut in just one three hour session (with overdubs), it still sounds tight, bright and packed with great ideas and inspired playing.

"That was quite a band," says Jack fondly. "It was also the beginning of my songwriting career."

Janet Godfrey, the band's fan club secretary, co-wrote songs like 'Baby Make Love To Me' and 'Baby Be Good To Me' with Jack. She later became the first Mrs Bruce.

By now, Jack had switched from double bass to bass guitar and in the process helped revolutionise the way rock musicians used the instrument. His full-toned, free-wheeling style was the precursor for today's heavy, funk bass. But he didn't get away with his innovations without some opposition.

Says Bruce: "The first time I played bass guitar was for a Jamaican jazz guitar player, Ernest Ranglin, who used me Graham, and Ginger to make an EP record. He wanted bass guitar, so I went and borrowed one from a music shop and immediately fell in love with it. I had been a snob about bass guitars but it was great. It was loud and easy to play. To get a slapping effect, I just applied my double bass technique."
The band went out on the road to work virtually seven nights a week. But they never saw much money for all their hard work. "We did three hundred gigs a year – which is quite incredible, considering we never got any money. Most of it went to the agency – and to Graham!"

Many thought Bruce should have been the lead singer with the band, but despite his feature spot on the rolling tumbling blues 'Traintime', which later became incorporated in Cream's set, Graham still hogged most of the vocals. "I didn't think of myself as a singer then. I just did back-up vocals and a slow blues. But I

suppose I started to get a taste for singing. It was actually due to Eric's encouragement that I started to sing later in Cream. Mainly because Eric didn't want to sing! There was a battle over who wasn't going to be the singer... I lost. We both suffered from the thing about singers not being musicians. We just wanted to be musicians who stood there playing – which is strange, now that Eric is known as a singer."

Their leader, the bulky and moustachioed Bond, was a powerful figure who encouraged his musicians to play at the best of their ability. He had made his name on the jazz scene, playing alto saxophone with the Don Rendell Quintet, and he had won the 1961 Melody Maker readers' poll, 'New Star' section. His conversion to the Hammond organ gave him extra power to blast audiences into submission, as his musical tastes veered away from Charlie Parker, Ornette Coleman and Eric Dolphy towards Ray Charles and Muddy Waters.

"The first time I played bass guitar was for a Jamaican jazz guitar player, Ernest Ranglin, who used me Graham, and Ginger to make an EP record. He wanted bass guitar, so I went and borrowed one from a music shop and immediately fell in love with it."

However, public tastes in 1965, then as now, veered towards the attractive and the commercial. That wasn't the only reason the Bond Organisation couldn't expect to crack the big time. Their music was bound up in saxophones and keyboards. However exciting the combination, the electric guitar was the lynchpin of rock music. Despite Jack's valiant efforts to turn the 6-string bass into a lead instrument, the band lacked a guitar hero. The most celebrated young guitarist of the day was firmly ensconced in the ranks of John Mayall's Bluesbreakers.

The Bond Organisation reached a peak and could go no further. Ginger Baker tired of living in poverty was determined to leave and form a successful group that would make money, and still retain its musical credibility. Jack Bruce had already quit Bond, after a row with Baker, and after a stint with John Mayall was earning more money to support his wife Janet by playing with the chart topping Manfred Mann group. "I quite enjoyed some of it, like the instrumental numbers we did, but it wasn't really my scene."

Deserted by his star players, Bond would regroup and battle on for some years, but sank into a terrible downward spiral of personal misfortune, culminating in his tragic and mysterious death under the wheels of a London underground train on May 8, 1974.

"The Bond band was frightening but people weren't ready for it," recalled Bruce. "The Beatles were the sort of thing the public wanted – a good looking young group. After Graham Bond, I joined John Mayall for a while. I'd had a big bust-up with Ginger, a big fight. Without any doubt I got the sack!"
Most of the frustration within the band was caused by the fact that they were struggling to play great music in the face of apathy and indifference. They had been playing the clubs for three years and still didn't really earn enough to support their families.

"The Bond band was frightening but people weren't ready for it, the Beatles were the sort of thing the public wanted – a good looking young group."

Bruce was only with Mayall for six weeks, but during that time he got to play with Eric Clapton.

"I hadn't really liked him so much when he was with The Yardbirds, but when I saw him with Mayall I saw why everyone dug him so much. When I came in Eric was just about to leave the band. I actually only remember playing one Mayall gig with him, but I am assured that there were more than that. I can only remember this very strange gig at Heathrow Airport in a hangar. It was a staff party. I don't remember any more. It was all a blur as there was so much going on in my personal life at the time."
Jack and Ginger were determined to sort out their careers and put their pent-up energy and talent to good use. The third man, who would complete the winning team, was about to enter their lives.

Chapter Three
ERIC'S BLUES CRUSADE

There had been guitar heroes before Eric Clapton. Jazz pioneers like Charlie Christian, Les Paul, Herb Ellis and Barney Kessell had all brought the electric guitar to prominence and shown its extraordinary versatility. There were the great blues guitarists like BB King, Freddie King and T-Bone Walker, while in rock'n'roll the sidemen who backed the stars also achieved considerable status like Scotty Moore with Elvis Presley, who was described in a biography of Elvis as: "The great unsung hero of Elvis Presley's life". In Britain during the early Sixties, Hank B Marvin of The Shadows became hugely popular and widely admired by aspiring teenage guitarists for his clean cut, original sound. The Shadows achieved unparalleled chart success with instrumental hits like 'Apache' that hit Number One in in the UK in July 1960. But their dominance would be swept away by the arrival of The Beatles, and then Cream.

Eric Patrick Clapton, the guitarist who did most to define the sound of modern rock music, was born in Ripley, Surrey, a village thirty miles south of London, on March 30, 1945. His birth and up-bringing reflected the upheavals caused by the Second World War. He was the son of Patricia Clapton and Edward Fryer, a Canadian soldier who had been stationed in England. Later Fryer, who was already married, went back to his wife in Canada. Patricia married another Canadian soldier and they both went off to Germany before settling in Canada. Eric was left in England in the care of his grandparents, Jack and Rose Clapp. Jack was a plasterer and bricklayer. Years later, at the height of his fame, Eric occasionally liked to refer to himself as a "musical labourer".

Clapton's grandparents didn't have much interest in music, although Rose always took a keen interest in his career and loved to hear him play.

Eric spent a quiet enough time at Ripley Primary School and later St. Bede's Secondary Modern.

When he was aged ten he started listening to pop music on the radio. One day a strangely powerful record called 'Fox Chase' by the blues duo Sonny Terry & Brownie McGhee was played on a children's radio programme.

It enthralled the young Clapton. He first saw a guitar being played when Jerry Lee Lewis and his band performed 'Great Balls Of Fire' on TV. Recalled Eric: 'It was like seeing someone from outer space. Here I was in this village that was never going to change, yet there on TV was something out of the future. And I wanted to go there!"

The 'guitar' Eric had seen on TV was a Fender bass guitar, but he didn't know the difference.

He decided to try and build his own guitar. It was quite a craze at a time when schoolboys were forming their own skiffle groups. Most of them made simple acoustic models, but Eric tried to carve a Stratocaster from a block of wood. He was defeated by the problem of creating the neck and frets.
Eric's grandparents doted on their boy and, as Eric says: "I was the only child in the family, and they used to spoil me something terrible. So I badgered them until they bought me a plastic Elvis Presley guitar."

The guitar wouldn't stay in tune, but at least Eric could put on his favourite Gene Vincent records and mime to them in the bedroom mirror.

ORIGINS

Eric enjoyed a happy childhood until one day when he was aged 12, his real mother turned up and he discovered the truth about his origins. It undermined his confidence and left him hurt and confused, especially as his mother had to be referred to as his 'sister'.

Said Eric later: "I was raised by my grandparents under the illusion that they were my parents, and so it was a kind of screwy set-up, which sorted itself out as I got older. But throughout my teens, I was very confused, angry and lonely."
At school he felt himself an outsider, and as a result was given a hard time by pupils and teachers alike. But eventually he found a clique of friends who shared his burgeoning interest in rock'n'roll.

Essentially a shy, sensitive and private person, he could easily be hurt and influenced by others. Yet he had an inner strength and a great sense of humour that delighted in the absurd.

He also had the ability to submerge himself in a role which, as a young man, enabled him to act out the part of a blues man – until he quite legitimately became one, accepted by his peers and even his own role models. His innate feeling for the blues, perhaps heightened by his own inner turmoil, gave his playing extraordinary strength, authenticity and conviction quite early on. There were louder, faster guitarists in the world, but none had the feeling and subtlety that Eric at his best would one day imbue in his playing.

His grandparents finally gave in to pressure and gave him his first proper guitar, a Hofner acoustic, when he was 15. He had heard an album by blues man Big Bill Broonzy that made a tremendous impression. "I'd never heard anything like it," he recalled.

"I was playing guitar all the time, teaching myself things, learning from records. At first I played exactly like Chuck Berry."

Playing the guitar like Big Bill proved much harder than he thought and he simply gave up trying. Understandably, his grandparents thought it was just another schoolboy craze that would be quickly forgotten. The neck of his guitar began to warp as it lay abandoned for a couple of years.

After leaving school in 1962, he enrolled at Kingston School Of Art to study stained-glass design. As he had been interested in drawing since the age of six, his grandparents encouraged him and he passed enough examinations to get a place. But Eric never really settled down to study.

His interest in the guitar revived when he heard records owned by fellow students. Their tastes veered towards the music of BB King, Muddy Waters, Howlin' Wolf and Chuck Berry. He also learned to appreciate the work of a uniquely different rocker – Buddy Holly. This sudden upsurge of interest in the blues among English youth took root most strongly in the art colleges. They became breeding grounds for musicians who helped create the great rock boom.

Eric didn't just want to play records. He got out his old guitar and began practising. It was his downfall as far as the college was concerned. He drank heavily, played records all day and did hardly any work. After three months he was asked to leave and was struck off the register. Said Clapton later: "Actually I am quite proud of that. Not many people are kicked out of art college. I was playing records most of the time and getting drunk in the pub at lunch time. I was an undesirable influence on the other students."

Clutching his trusty acoustic guitar, Clapton spent his days busking around Kingston and Richmond, earning a reputation as the local hobo. He took a job for a while working as a labourer with his grandfather, but most of the time was spent learning how to master his guitar and making trips up to London and the West End.

He hung around in coffee bars and met people like Long John Baldry who played 12-string guitar and sang folk and blues. He got deeper into the blues discovering the music of Blind Lemon Jefferson, Son House and Skip James.

"I was playing guitar all the time, teaching myself things, learning from records. At first I played exactly like Chuck Berry." Then Eric got into the works of Robert Johnson and Blind Boy Fuller while he retained his love for Big Bill Broonzy. One of the first songs he learned was Broonzy's 'Walk Down The Lonesome Road'.

He also listened to Otis Rush and Blind Willie Johnson, then a friend played him an album featuring historic recordings by Robert Johnson called 'King Of The Delta Blues Singers'. Clapton was shocked by what he heard: "I couldn't take it. I thought it was really non-musical, very raw. Then I went back to it later, and got into it. At the first hearing, though, it was just too much anguish to take."

Finally he discovered BB King and, said Clapton: "When I came out of it, I was developing in a Chicago blues vein. But you can never reach the standards of the original, and after a while I knew I had to develop my own style. I would play something I heard on record and then add something of my own. Gradually my own things took over more and more."

The next step was to join a band and he teamed up with a new found friend, guitarist Tom McGuinness, who would eventually achieve fame in Manfred Mann and went on to form McGuinness Flint.

They met at the Station Hotel Richmond and formed a band called The Roosters. It was 1963 when Eric was just 18-years-old. They started out playing at pubs and at parties for friends. The Roosters lasted from January to September and was probably the first full-time British R&B group. They used to play John Lee Hooker's 'Boom Boom' and Muddy Waters' 'Hoochie Coochie Man'.

Tom McGuinness recalls the pioneering days with great fondness. "The Sixties were a magic period for us. Pop music then was accessible to a wide age group. The Beatles appealed to all ages – until John took up with that Yoko woman!"

LIFE WITH THE ROOSTERS

As R&B began to challenge the dominance of pop music, there was some scepticism. Blues fans like Clapton and McGuinness were still in a tiny minority and most people had never heard of the original Black American artists they raved about.

Says McGuinness: "I can remember when I wanted to go off and play R&B these guys were saying: 'You're mad, you'll be back in six months. No-one wants to hear that sort of music'. I had to find other people who knew about John Lee Hooker. I saw an advert that said: 'Pianist wants to join rhythm & blues band'. I wrote to him and met the guy. It was Ben Palmer, who was trying to get a band together with Paul Jones. We kept in touch, and meanwhile a girlfriend introduced me to Eric Clapton. Ben, Eric and I formed The Roosters which lasted about nine months."

The rest of the Roosters were Robin Mason on drums and Terry Brennan (vocals).

Tom was the second guitarist and says: "We never recorded and we couldn't find a bass player, which illustrates how few people there were wanting to play R&B in 1963."

Eric made the switch from acoustic to electric to play with The Roosters and bought himself a Kay model guitar that he'd seen advertised. He had learned how to bend strings to alter notes and developed a 'singing' quality by using very light strings.

He kept breaking them during numbers and while he re-strung his guitar, audiences would begin a slow handclap, which resulted in his nickname 'Slowhand Clapton'.

The Roosters broke up due to lack of money and commitment from some of the band. Eric occasionally jammed with Alexis Korner at his Ealing Blues Club and then joined another group. Says Tom: "Eric and I went to play with a guy from Liverpool called Casey Jones. That lasted only six weeks, then Eric joined The Yardbirds and I got the call to join Manfred Mann on bass." "Casey Jones and the Engineers was a very heavy pop show and I couldn't stand that for very long," said Eric. "At that time I was such a purist and they were playing real Top Twenty stuff which was disastrous."

Eric's next move would help establish his name as a top lead guitar player, even though he wasn't entirely happy with the results.

"We never recorded and we couldn't find a bass player, which illustrates how few people there were wanting to play R&B in 1963."

The Rolling Stones had soared to ascendancy during the first frantic months of the R&B boom. Then in 1963 they left the Crawdaddy Club, at the Station Hotel, Richmond where they had built-up a fanatical following. The Stones were destined for greater things, and were replaced by the Yardbirds, fronted by singer Keith Relf. The band had grown out of an outfit called the Metropolitan Blues quartet, made up of Kingston Art college students who played local pubs and clubs. They had made their debut as the Yardbirds at a unique venue, a hotel on Eel Pie Island, in the middle of the River Thames. The band's guitarist was Anthony 'Top' Topham and the rest of the group included Chris Dreja (rhythm guitar), Paul Samwell-Smith (bass) and Jim McCarty (drums). Anthony was replaced by Eric Clapton a few weeks after the band's arrival at the Crawdaddy Club. Eric went to see them and was pretty scornful of Topham's limited technique. "I was watching them one week and playing with them the next," he recalls.

Topham was a blues enthusiast but he found the role of lead guitarist too demanding and he suffered considerable parental opposition. When he quit, Keith phoned Eric, who he had known at art school. They had previously talked about forming a group together.

Eric came down for a rehearsal at the South Western Hotel and quickly fitted in with the band's blues policy. He was a much more advanced player than Topham and knew many more numbers, so his arrival gave the fledgling Yardbirds a big boost.

"I had only been with Casey Jones & The Engineers for three or four weeks when the Yardbirds asked me to go along to the Crawdaddy to listen to them and have a chat," said Clapton later. "I'd heard the group were interested in me joining them, so I went to the Crawdaddy, looked in and thought: 'What's this?' They were playing things like 'Can't Judge A Book' like R&B puppets. I thought it would be a cushy job, so I joined them. Eventually I got quite brainwashed with this commercial R&B."

Under the tutelage of a wild-eyed Rasputin-style manager, Giorgio Gomelsky, the Yardbirds began a chequered but mostly successful and highly-influential career. Giorgio was an emotional but enthusiastic man who loved the blues and encouraged his young charges. He was a Russian with a Swiss passport and spoke several different languages. He was a larger-than-life figure who recorded many of the pioneer British acts – often without their knowledge or permission – but he left a great musical legacy for historians.

For all his faults, which included driving cars the wrong way along one-way streets and talking anyone within earshot into the ground, he pushed the nervous suburban youths into achieving their musical potential. It was his ambition to make the Yardbirds even bigger than The Stones... and for a while it looked as if they might succeed.

As well as producing hits like 'For Your Love', 'Heart Full Of Soul' and 'Evil Hearted You', the band also became known as the hothouse that nurtured three of the greatest rock guitarists of all time – Clapton and his successors Jeff Beck and Jimmy Page. The Yardbirds propelled Clapton into the limelight and got him on record and out on tour. However, he always felt ambivalent about his role in the band. He enjoyed the attention during his first year on board – apart from the Stones and Manfred Mann, the Yardies were one of the most successful bands of the period – yet he became unsettled about his own playing and doubts began to creep in. Sometimes he was so shy about his guitar playing that he wouldn't take any solos and would try to hide behind his amplifier. Then, as his experience and technique improved, so did his confidence.

"I had only been with Casey Jones & The Engineers for three or four weeks when the Yardbirds asked me to go along to the Crawdaddy to listen to them and have a chat. I'd heard the group were interested in me joining them, so I went to the Crawdaddy, looked in and thought: 'What's this?' They were playing things like 'Can't Judge A Book' like R&B puppets. I thought it would be a cushy job, so I joined them. Eventually I got quite brainwashed with this commercial R&B."

I met Eric for the first time in October 1964, not long after I joined the Melody Maker. An interview was scheduled for The Yardbirds and we assembled in the Kardomah coffee bar in Fleet Street. It was the first occasion I'd talked to a full group in-person, and quickly learned it was a bad idea to try and interview five people at once – they distract each other, indulge in in-jokes and badinage, and there is always one who is too shy to talk, and probably has the most interesting things to say, while the noisiest make mock of the whole ordeal. Then there is the usual problem of their insulting waitresses and creating 'a scene'.

73

In fact The Yardbirds were generally pleasant and well-behaved, although I noticed that Eric was the most sensible and tended to smile at the exuberant prattle going on around him. The band had just released their second single 'Good Morning Little Schoolgirl' (a follow-up to 'I Wish You Would') and The Yardbirds were nervous about the effect having a hit single might have on their credibility with blues fans. The headline on the subsequent piece was 'Oh No! Not A Hit Disc'. It was just the angle the MM wanted, although it probably gave the band's management and record company palpitations.

The story ran: "A successful future is staring The Yardbirds right in the face – and it worries them! They're worried about losing the thousands of faithful rhythm and blues fans they have attracted – without the aid of a single hit record."

It was true the band a few problems. Their singer Keith Relf had recently collapsed with a perforated lung and the band had been out of action for months. The single had been recorded the previous March. But they had kept a grip on their all-important fan following, as Eric was keen to explain: "Club audiences are very possessive and when records start selling the kids come up to you and say: 'We've lost you'. We left the Crawdaddy for a while to do a tour with Billy J Kramer. When we played the Crawdaddy again it wasn't quite the same. Now we play at The Marquee and it's a complete rave. But we are worried like hell that we'll lose R&B fans if we get a hit record. We like pop fans, but we want both. We would look upon it as our biggest achievement if we could be the most popular band in the country without a hit record. But we are tired of the snobs who say they don't like an artist any more because he has a hit record. Why is it criminal to be successful? People actually say they don't like Chuck Berry any more because everybody else likes him – they've got to like somebody else. They don't like Hambone Willy Kneebone anymore – everybody has heard of him – so they say they like Rabbit Foot Walker instead!"

I liked all of the Yardbirds, particularly the frail and overwrought Keith Relf, but Eric was the one who gained most people's respect. He was both witty and charming and it was sad to see his early enthusiasm for the band eroded.

I went to see them at the Marquee – it may have been the same day of the interview – and saw the crowds of fans lining Wardour Street. Their performance was a flurry of shaking maracas, yelling blues vocals, and frantic drumming, while Eric's guitar was used to build up a crescendo of noise on a long version of 'Smokestack Lightning' in a style known as a rave up,

a precursor of the freak out, when all inhibitions are lost in a maelstrom of noise and rhythm. The excitement The Yardbirds created at The Marquee was partially captured on their album 'Five Live Yardbirds' (Columbia), recorded in March 1964 and released in January 1965. They had actually recorded an earlier album, with authentic American blues singer Sonny Boy Williamson, at the Crawdaddy club in October 1963, but it was not released until a couple of years later in January 1966. It was Giorgio's idea to lumber the Yardbirds with old Sonny Boy who drank lots of whiskey and terrified the English lads. He later went back home and told how none of them could play the blues. At least they could all play in the same key together.

The Yardbirds had indeed won a fanatical following during their early years and Eric Clapton's reputation as a star soloist spread across the country. His solos on such driving tunes as 'I Wish You Would' caused a sensation. But the rest of the Yardbirds, notably Paul Samwell-Smith, the bass player, wanted the band to move on from the blues to experiment with songwriting and new recording techniques. Eric never seemed to share this enthusiasm and became a somewhat enigmatic figure as far as the rest were concerned. When the band wanted to wear long hair, he kept his short. While the others smiled cheerfully in photographs, he scowled at the camera. He was constantly changing his image. One minute he was a mod and wore bouffant hair-dos. Then he become a moustachioed beatnik. It certainly helped to keep people guessing and ensured his photo file was invariably out of date.

I went to watch them recording 'For Your Love' at IBC Studios, London in December 1964. It was the first time I'd been in a recording studio. In those days this was the equivalent of gaining entry to Buckingham Palace or the inner sanctums of the BBC. It was fun to watch them devise 'For Your Love' with organist Brian Auger playing harpsichord and Denny Piercy adding bongos. It was a clever imaginative pop production, but Eric grew increasingly uncomfortable with the direction the band was taking. The Yardbirds were always arguing and resented their manager treating them like naughty children.

Eric confessed later: "Playing with The Yardbirds put me in a very strange frame of mind. I was all screwed up about my playing and I'd lost a lot of my original values. My attitude within the group got really sour and it was kind of hinted that it would be better for me to leave. I was withdrawing into myself, becoming intolerable, really dogmatic."

The Yardbirds with Eric (far left)

ERIC QUITS

O n their interminable round of gigs, the band wound up at the Bromel Club in Bromley, not far from where I lived in south London. Bands played in a small back room of the Bromley Court Hotel, and virtually every great group of the day ended up there. On the night I went to see The Yardbirds I could sense there was something wrong. Eric looked really miserable on stage and couldn't wait to jump off at the end of the set that hadn't gone down particularly well. 'Smokestack Lightning', usually a crowd-pleasing routine, had received minimal applause from a clutch of people more concerned with getting served at the bar. "You look fed up," I observed. "You noticed," said Eric with heavy irony. But he smiled and seemed pleased that somebody cared. Not long after he quit the group.

"Playing with The Yardbirds put me in a very strange frame of mind. I was all screwed up about my playing and I'd lost a lot of my original values. My attitude within the group got really sour and it was kind of hinted that it would be better for me to leave. I was withdrawing into myself, becoming intolerable, really dogmatic."

Said Eric: "I was fooled into joining the group. I fooled myself, attracted by the pop thing, the big money, the little chicks. It wasn't until I had been doing it for 18 months that I started to take my music seriously. I realised that I wanted to be doing it for the rest of my life, so I had better start doing it right."

These were admirable, mature motives, even though they probably seemed simply wilful and perverse at a time when most musicians were desperate for a taste of stardom. Eric genuinely felt that his early commitment to the blues was being compromised. There were other reasons. The Yardbirds tied Eric down musically. They tried to rein in his guitar solos which, as they became more wild and extrovert, created more excitement among audiences than Keith Relf's vocals and harmonica playing which tended to dominate their recordings. The band had a tiger by the tail and wouldn't let him loose.

"The Yardbirds were tying me down," he explained. "I wanted to get a step further on and they wanted more discipline. I was all screwed up about my playing and didn't like anything I did." Eric particularly hated 'For Your Love', and left just before it was released in March 1965.

He told my Melody Maker colleague Nick Jones: "It was only when I got on stage away from all the hubble bubble that I suddenly realised I didn't really like what the group did or played. The whole thing became so business-like we became more like machines than human beings."

When he joined his next band he had a chance to show just what he could achieve given his head. First came a confused period of mystery and rumour. What was Eric going to do next? He considered becoming a painter and giving up music. Then came a call from John Mayall, the Manchester born leader of The Bluesbreakers. Here was an outfit dedicated to the blues with an almost frightening intensity. Mayall played keyboards and guitar and sang in a rather nasal but sincere fashion. His band was a big draw on the club circuit but they became even bigger when Eric joined, replacing lead guitarist Roger Dean in May 1965.

"I knew Mayall's music and had a soft spot for him and I just made up my mind to join him because I thought it was the only thing to do," said Eric.

Even here Eric was restricted and only got two 12 bar solos a night to express himself. Also life with the Mayall band wasn't exactly fun and games. The leader had a rather puritanical, parsimonious outlook, and while it was probably sensible to ban drink, it was a bit unfair to expect his band to sleep in the van! Eric explained how he wound up in the Bluesbreakers.

"I'd seen them at The Flamingo and wasn't really that keen on them because I never really thought John had a lot of control over his voice. And John had many quirks. Bands, when they've got a leader, often gang up against him behind his back and in The Bluesbreakers we used to really take the piss out of him behind his back on stage. John was an amazing man. No-one was allowed to drink! John McVie got slung out of the band's van halfway between Birmingham and London one night because he was drunk and he had to make his own way home. Also he had his own bunk bed in the van did John, and you had to sit upright in the front while he got into bed in the back. If we did a gig in Manchester where his parents lived, he'd go and stay the night at his mum's and we'd have to sleep in the van. He didn't get you a hotel, so there were disadvantages being in that band!"

Clapton became restless and rather envied his friends from art school who led a carefree Bohemian existence that wasn't tied down to a rigid touring schedule. He put together a fun group that called themselves The Glands and set off on what was described as "a trip round the world". They got as far as Greece where they ran out of money.

"I was living with some pretty mad people, just drinking wine all day and listening to jazz and blues," said Eric. "We decided to pool our money, buy an estate car and take off round the world. The job with Mayall had become a job and I wanted to go and have some fun. So we ended in Greece, playing blues." They met a club proprietor who hired Eric and his mates to open for a Greek band that played Beatles songs. Tragically the Greek band was involved in a road accident and half the band were killed. Clapton, obliged to play with both bands, quickly learned all the Beatles and Kinks songs in their set.

"It was only when I got on stage away from all the hubble bubble that I suddenly realised I didn't really like what the group did or played. The whole thing became so business-like we became more like machines than human beings."

Then Eric realised he was trapped and the proprietor wouldn't let him go. He fired the rest of Eric's band and kept his clever young British guitarist to play with the Greek band. He confiscated his guitar as insurance. After a couple of weeks, Eric managed to escape by saying he had to re-string it. As soon as he got his guitar back, he fled. He came back to England to rejoin the Bluesbreakers and there were sighs of relief from his British fans.

His second period with the Bluesbreakers ran from November 1965 to June 1966, during which time Eric began to get more seriously involved with his own music and playing. Audiences marvelled at the way he poured his feelings into his playing and the fluency of his technique. He was never flashy, always melodic, and they loved him to the extent that fans began to refer to him simply as "God". There were cries of "Give God a solo!" at gigs. Slogans began to appear on walls round town proclaiming "Clapton is God".

I went to see Eric playing with Mayall at the Zeeta Rooms, a club in Putney, and thought that he looked rather menacing in his moustache and sideburns. The merry mod of The Yardbirds had been replaced by a serious blues dude. I got the impression that he still wasn't entirely happy in the tightly disciplined Mayall set-up. Given a chance though, he played up a storm and the fans hung onto every note.

The album he cut with Mayall during this period became a classic and a surprise best seller. 'Bluesbreakers: John Mayall With Eric Clapton' (Decca) was produced by Mike Vernon and released in July 1966. It featured some of Eric's best playing and is still regarded by die-hard fans as his best work on record. His guitar flies with exuberant confidence, and even though Mayall's band could not match Cream or Blind Faith, their tight discipline and lower musical goals meant that Clapton's playing shone through the backing. There was a feminine, lyrical quality to his playing that was not far removed from the 'woman tone' ideal promulgated by BB King who dubbed his own guitar "Lucille".

On tracks like 'All Your Love', 'Hideaway' and the club-goers favourite showcase number, 'Steppin' Out', Eric delivered some of the best guitar work of the period. His playing was both imaginative and subtle and not even the strangled vocals and uneven drumming from his team mates could detract from the sound of Clapton at his youthful best.

The album quickly became a 'must' in any collection and even the cover became a classic, showing Eric calmly reading The Beano children's comic, with a wry smile, while the rest of the band gazed mournfully at the camera.

As well as playing on the 12 tracks on the 'Bluesbreakers' album, Eric also appeared with Mayall on such items as 'I'm Your Witch Doctor' and 'Telephone Blues' and he recorded some material with Jimmy Page, which appeared on the Immediate label on the albums 'Blues Anytime Vols. 1 & 2'. The latter tracks that included 'Tribute To Elmore' and 'Draggin' My Tail' weren't particularly inspired, and weren't originally intended for release, but they showed Clapton and Page relaxing before they were both caught up in the madness of Cream and Led Zeppelin. More important was a track called 'Lonely Years' a Mayall-Clapton collaboration with vocals, harmonica and guitar, featured on the 'Raw Blues' (Decca) album eventually released in 1967. It managed to obtain the most authentic blues sound ever captured in a British studio. However, it wasn't the most commercial nor necessarily the most exciting.

Re-creating Chicago blues was something of a crusade for Mayall but it wasn't a sufficiently satisfying mode of expression for Clapton. Contemporary rock music was growing and changing and offering all kinds of possibilities. This was the age of Bob Dylan and The Beatles and there was much more music to play and explore.

There was always the possibility that Clapton could be much more than a featured lead guitarist in a local club band. He could be a writer, a singer and all-round performer. In the mid-Sixties there was a great build-up of frustrated talent and the dam seemed about to burst.

On the club scene there was a network of musicians who all got to know each other as they played an endless round of 'one-nighters' and travelled the motorway networks in battered vans, living on a diet of egg and chips. There was much coveting of other musicians, while the top band leaders tried to keep a lid on plots and escape bids. Whenever musicians gathered in their favourite pubs like The Ship in Wardour Street, Soho, the talk was invariably how to get into a band like John Mayall's Bluesbreakers – or how to get out of it!

One arrival in the ranks was Jack Bruce, seeking sanctuary from the Graham Bond Organisation. Clapton was immediately struck by the power of his bass playing and his vocal style. Recalled Eric later: "I knew how good he was from then on. He sang a couple of things and they were really great. He was a natural first choice for any group I might dream about forming. I hit it off with Jack really well. Then he left to go with Manfred Mann and John got John McVie back. I decided that playing with Jack was more exciting. There was something creative there. Most of what we were doing with Mayall was imitating the records we'd got, but Jack had something else. He had no reverence for what we were doing and was composing new parts as he went along. I had never heard that before and it took me someplace else. I thought, well if he could do that, and I could, we could get a drummer... I could be Buddy Guy with a composing bass player. And that's how Cream came about."

During his tenure with Mayall, Jack cut a version of 'Stormy Monday Blues' with Eric that was included on the LP 'John Mayall Looking Back' (Decca) released in 1969.

CREAM DREAM

When Bruce arrived in the Bluesbreakers, Eric sensed that here was a kindred spirit who might help him find a way out of the Mayall formula. But the bassist had stayed only a few weeks before going off to join Manfred Mann in search of his fortune. Eric was on his own again and feeling depressed and frustrated. He knew he was a good guitarist even if he was uneasy about the adulation. He just needed a clear direction. He told Nick Jones in March 1966:

"I think the only way is to go to America. Forming a blues band in England is like banging your head against a brick wall. Nobody wants to record it. I'm not interested in guitar sound and technique, but in people and what you can do to them via music. I'm very conceited and I think I have a power and my guitar is a medium for expressing that power. I don't need people to say how good I am, I've worked it out by myself. It's nothing to do with technique and rehearsing, it is to do with the person behind that guitar who is trying to find an outlet. My guitar is a medium through which I can make contact to myself. It's very lonely."

Then one night in June 1966, when the Bluesbreakers were playing a gig in Oxford, it seemed the loneliness and frustration could be overcome.

The explosive, forceful Ginger Baker arrived unannounced and asked if he could jam with the band. Within a few bars of the powerhouse drummer taking over, Eric knew they could work together. It seemed obvious they shouldn't waste the opportunity that was staring them in the face. At the end of the set, the two sat together silently and had a drink. Ginger then fixed Eric with his twinkling, penetrating stare and said: "How about getting a group together?"

Eric thought it was telepathy at work. He already knew what his ideal group would be like. It would feature himself with Ginger Baker... and Jack Bruce. When Baker made his proposal Eric just said: "Yes... what about Jack?" The drummer thought for a moment and then agreed that Jack was the only possible choice. He would go round and look up his old partner and see if they could bury the hatchet. Jack needed no further persuasion.

Says Jack: "Ginger came round to my first wife Janet's parents' house. He asked if I would join him to help form the new band. He had already approached Eric and he'd said yes, but he wanted me to be the singer in the band. I had only recently fallen out with Ginger. You see we were very close in many ways, and I sort of regarded him as my older brother. Like a lot of people who are very close, it's very easy to get up each other's nose. But the main reasons were musical. When I was playing acoustic bass, Ginger liked it, because he never really liked loud music... ha, ha! That's funny because he was the loudest drummer I'd ever heard. But dynamics have changed so much over the years that Ginger is now a quiet drummer really. He's obviously very different from today's drummers who just put out back beats. Once I started to experiment with more melodic lines on bass guitar, he felt that was wrong. He felt I should be playing in a much more simple style. That's why we fell out. But around that time we had played with the American singer Marvin Gaye on TV and he was very encouraging to me.

He came round to my place in Hampstead and we spent the whole night talking and he actually asked me to go back and join his band in the States. But I couldn't do it, because I was still with Graham. But it encouraged me to carry on developing my bass style. I had been influenced by James Jamieson, who played bass in a very melodic style on the early Tamla Motown records. The lead and bass lines did counter melodies and that really impressed me. Meeting Marvin Gaye was a real turning point. If it hadn't been for him, I might have given up bass guitar and gone back to playing acoustic bass in a jazz context where I could get away with a lot more."

It was a dispute over Jack's right to free expression that really sparked the notorious bust-up with Baker. Says Jack: "We came to blows a couple of times. There was a gig in Golders Green when we really fell out. It was a terrible night when he was hitting me on the head with drum sticks and I threw my bass at him and demolished his drum kit. We ended up rolling all over the floor. The rest of the band came and got us apart and took us out of separate doors. Then I left the band. It must have been quite a thing for Ginger to come back and ask me to join him with Eric, and obviously I was very pleased to try it."
All they needed now was a name for the proposed new group. Eric had a great idea. They were the cream of the crop. Why be modest? They should call themselves... The Cream.

Chapter Four
CREAM OF THE CROP

Eric Clapton devised the name Cream in an inspired moment, the day the group played together for the first time. The historic meeting took place in Ginger Baker's front room, at his home in the North London suburb of Neasden. They set up their equipment and lost themselves in a long improvisation which proved that they had an extraordinary musical empathy.

Recalls Jack Bruce: "It was a tiny little room and we played all afternoon – it was magical."

"We came to blows a couple of times. Then I left the band. It must have been quite a thing for Ginger to come back and ask me to join him with Eric, and obviously I was very pleased to try it."

The day before they had held a planning meeting at Eric's flat, which later transferred to a nearby park, where they had a smoke and dreamed of conquering the world. It was a good opportunity for the three to get to know each other better. Jack and Ginger were still liable to fly off the handle and Eric was a bit alarmed when he discovered there had been a problem between them. However, it was felt that Clapton, with his mild and affable personality, could be the peace maker. Certainly they could present a united front and there was a shared sense of humour and purpose. They were all too excited about the idea and the prospects of the band to allow petty squabbles to spoil their enterprise.

The most pressing, urgent problem was to find some material. It was obvious that they couldn't sustain a band on a few blues jams. "We didn't really know what kind of material we wanted to play," says Jack. "I hadn't written anything apart from a couple of things for Graham and a couple of strange things I'd done for my own single. Originally Eric thought it was going to be a blues band and our original repertoire was going to be standard blues."

It wasn't long after Ginger phoned me with the news of the band that I was invited down to see them play at the church hall, where Robert Stigwood nervously surveyed his charges and quietly asked me: "Are they any good?"

The band were in the throes of playing traditional blues at the time, Ginger executing snare drum rolls in the style of his hero, the New Orleans drummer Baby Dodds. It sounded wonderful to me, but may have worried Robert, who was probably hoping for something a little more commercial.

Stigwood was a pop entrepreneur who would eventually become one of the most powerful figures in the recording and entertainment business, and ultimately one of the richest men in the world. Brought up in Adelaide, South Australia, he at one time contemplated becoming a Catholic priest, before ending up working for an advertising agency. He arrived in Britain in 1956, having travelled in India and Aden en route. In 1962 he began working in a talent agency for actors and later helped one of his clients, John Leyton, to become a pop singer, with the assistance of pioneer independent record producer Joe Meek. Leyton scored an instant smash hit with 'Johnny Remember Me' and had several more chart toppers, which helped establish Stigwood's first publishing and management empire.

But after a disastrous Chuck Berry tour which Robert promoted, his company went into liquidation with debts of nearly forty thousand pounds. Despite this setback, he had set up his own Reaction label, did a deal with Polydor for distribution and signed Cream as his first act in a campaign to rebuild his business. Subsequently the Robert Stigwood Organisation set up their own RSO label, and Robert also had tremendous success with the Bee Gees and later with hit shows and movies like Saturday Night Fever.

Jack Bruce explains that it was Ginger Baker's idea to ask Robert to be their manager. "It was very much Ginger's band in the early days. Certainly the business decisions were left to Ginger while the artistic decisions were more Eric's, in the sense that he would decide on album covers and the choice of clothes. It was Ginger's decision to bring in Stigwood, and I was against it because I didn't think we should have a manager. We had a good agent in Robert Masters. We just needed a good accountant and I felt we could manage ourselves. But Ginger didn't agree with that and thought we should have 'Stiggy' and I thought that was the most unfortunate decision. It was mismanagement that caused the premature collapse of the band. It was just down to greed and lack of belief in the band,

88

and the failure to understand just how good it was. Stigwood didn't think it would last anyway and the idea was to milk it while it was happening. If we'd had a bit more time and care spent on us, instead of being constantly put on the road, we could have had a month or two off to go and write material together. We never had any real time to do that. A lot of the bitterness that came in later might have been avoided."

But there was no bitterness, only optimism and good humour the day of the first rehearsal. I must admit, I was filled with eager anticipation and felt very privileged to hear the band at such an early stage at such close quarters. It was hard to believe that here were Clapton, Baker & Bruce working out their destiny in such a mundane setting. There was that strange smell peculiar to all church halls of dust, green baize and body odour, mostly the result of strenuous physical activity by boy scouts, or in this case, the dreaded Brownies. There was Ginger, fag pasted on his lower lip, concentrating ferociously on his drum beats, and Jack sporting a quizzical smile as he contemplated the chord changes. Eric floated around, his sideboards bristling, a guitar slung at the hip. On that summer day long ago, I asked him how he felt, bearing in mind the whole world was watching and waiting for them. "Nervous, very nervous."

Even with Ginger using only a snare and bass drums, the volume in the hall was deafening. He assured me that when they started gigging, he'd be using seven drums, including double bass drums.

"We've only got about a sixth of the gear here," Eric told me, "so you can imagine what it's going to sound like with full amplification and Ginger's tom toms as well."

The band stood around in a sea of cigarette ends and prepared to run through a few numbers for me, the band's first ever audience – or audient as Ronnie Scott might say.
Ginger, sporting a villainous looking beard, crouched low at his drums, ready to strike cymbals that were hung on almost vertically on their stands. Jack, wearing brown lace-up boots and with a harmonica harness around his neck, gripped his bass guitar, ready for Eric to count them in. Eric, wearing white bell-bottom trousers, was momentarily distracted by the sight of some girl fans hanging around outside and he paused to shout a few coarse cries at them. Then he counted in the first eruption of noise.

Eric and Jack sang in harmony, and then the harmonica wailed in harmony with the lead guitar. It seemed almost frightening. Compared to the worthy sounds of John Mayall's Bluesbreakers or even the Yardbirds at full tilt, this was like Armageddon. Perhaps The Who created more dynamic, spontaneous excitement but in terms of sheer, solid power and blistering instrumental attack, it was true to say there had been nothing like it heard on the planet. This was heavy rock at the instant of creation, a kind of super nova explosion which is still radiating outwards.

Ginger, armed with a huge pair of drum sticks, suggested they did their 'comedy number' for my benefit. This proved to be a jugband tune called 'Take Your Finger Off It' with a chord sequence similar to the old trad jazz number 'Ja Da'.
At the end, Eric looked at Jack and grinned: "You mucked up the end."

"Yes, I did, didn't I," said Jack coolly.

I never heard the band play the number again. The chaps then decided on a very British tea break and the trio drove off in their hired van, with me squashed in the front seat. Jack drove and pulled out into a main road without looking, and escaped colliding with a high speed car by a few seconds and fewer centimetres. I never forgot the look Ginger gave Jack, but nothing was said. Meanwhile Jack managed to block the main road traffic in both directions while attempting to complete a U-turn. Fortunately our nerves had been calmed by the powerful cigarettes we'd been smoking, just to ward off such moments of tension. It wasn't until I woke up the following morning, that I contemplated we might all have been 'totalled' and I wouldn't have been around to write the obituary. Meanwhile, the band adjourned to a nearby cafe where they talked enthusiastically about Cream's prospects and musical policy.

Everyone wanted to talk at once. "It's Blues Ancient and Modern," said Eric.

"We call it Sweet'n'Sour Rock'n'Roll," added Jack.

"Yes, that's a good headline," said Eric. "Pete Townshend is enthusiastic and he may write a number for us."

"At the moment we're trying to get a repertoire up for all the gigs we've got to do," said Ginger. "We're digging back as far as we can, even to 1927."

Jack told me that they planned to do one number called 'Long Haired Unsquare Dude Called Jack,' which Paul Jones used to sing with Manfred Mann. Again, nothing came of this plan. I asked them if they planned to play any music with a jazz feel, bearing in mind the Baker and Bruce background.

"I'd say jazz was definitely out," said Eric firmly. "Sweet'n'sour rock is definitely in. Most people have formed the impression of us as three solo musicians clashing with each other. We want to cancel that idea and be a group that plays together."

"If we'd had a bit more time and care spent on us, instead of being constantly put on the road, we could have had a month or two off to go and write material together. We never had any real time to do that. A lot of the bitterness that came in later might have been avoided."

The group were getting restless and when I asked them what sort of presentation they planned for their up-coming debut at the Windsor Jazz & Blues Festival, Eric replied: "We want a turkey on stage while we are playing. We all like turkeys and it's nice to have them around. I was going to have this hat made of a brim with a cage on top with a live frog inside. It would also be very nice to have stuffed bears on stage. We'd ignore them and not acknowledge their presence at all."

It seemed to me that young Master Clapton was not taking his responsibilities too seriously but his jokey answers reflected a need to defuse the build-up of tension before their debut. In any case Eric always had a great sense of humour and loved The Goons and the Bonzo Dog Doo Dah Band. In later years he befriended the Bonzos' famed tap dancer and drummer, Legs Larry Smith, and took him around on tour as a court jester. In the event, the hat with the frog failed to materialise, but Cream did cart its stuffed bear around on gigs. Whether anybody in the audience noticed it or not is hard to say. Maybe they thought he was the roadie.

Some ten days after the rehearsal, Cream played a secret warm-up gig at the Twisted Wheel Club, Manchester which I missed when my normally reliable network of spies let me down. But I went to see them play before an ecstatic crowd in the pouring rain at the National Jazz And Blues Festival on July 31, 1966. I spent most of my time in my Ford Consul sheltering from the rain, and trying to watch The Who and Georgie Fame through the sweep of windscreen wipers. But when The Cream came on, I leapt out into the mud and joined the thousands of fans who cheered the new band's debut.

They kicked off with 'Spoonful', the old Willie Dixon blues, and then tore straight into Jack Bruce's feature number, 'Traintime'. Eric played with such power that the fans continued to shout for more – even when he was actually playing more!

The warmth and enthusiasm of the reception seemed to stun the band. They were ready to celebrate when they arrived at a late night party held in their honour at Robert Stigwood's flat near Regents Park. That is, all of them were having a good time except Eric, who sat on the floor in a corner looking rather sad and miserable. Robert Stigwood was so concerned he asked me to go over and speak to Eric to find out what was the matter. I crouched beside him and I discovered he was in much the same mood that he'd been with The Yardbirds in their last days. It seemed he just wasn't happy with the musical direction of the new band.

It may have been the restless intensity of the playing, the feeling that he had to compete constantly with the other two for space, or simply the pressure on him from audiences to walk on water every time he plugged in a guitar. Whatever the truth of the matter, I tried to cheer Eric up and in any case he probably realised it was too late to call a halt. Cream's wheels of fire were in motion and the juggernaut had to run its course.

The band launched into a series of relatively small club dates, playing at such venues as Cooks Ferry Inn, North London, The Marquee (on August 16), The Manor House, The Ram Jam Club, and, of course, The Flamingo, home of Britain's R&B groups. They broke all attendance records and fans queued for seven hours to see them at The Marquee.

Clapton still had the biggest name, as a result of his album with John Mayall doing so well in the charts, so the new band was invariably billed as 'Cream featuring Eric Clapton'. Nobody minded too much, even though the whole concept was a band of equals.

But when they later arrived in America, some record executives got hold of the wrong end of the stick. They thought it was purely 'The Eric Clapton Group'.

This left Jack Bruce, as the main composer, feeling somewhat miffed.

"I still don't get recognition from people like Ahmet Ertegun, boss of Atlantic," says Bruce. "Cream was very much regarded as Eric's band with two backing musicians. He still does think that, because he made this very strange and insulting speech at the Rock'N'Roll Hall Of Fame induction ceremony in 1993, when he just talked about how Eric had this band called Cream It was very hurtful for Ginger because it was Ginger's idea and very much his band. Of course Ahmet didn't see it that way at all. He thought it was Eric's band."

It was an attitude that had been established right from the beginning, and what particularly bugged Bruce was the attitude towards his songs.

"I came up with things like 'Sunshine Of Your Love' and 'White Room' and Ertegun would say, 'No, that's no good, it's psychedelic hogwash, and anyway you shouldn't be singing, Eric has to be the lead singer. You're just the bass player'."

Bruce says a piece like 'White Room' came under fire because it was written in 5/4 time instead of the usual 4/4. Other songs were disregarded or cannibalised, like 'Strange Brew' on the band's second album 'Disraeli Gears'.

Says Jack: "It was grafted onto a backing track we had already recorded for 'Hey Lawdie Mama'. If you listen to it, you'll notice that the bass part is wrong because it's for a different song. They just sent Felix Pappalardi, the producer, a backing track which became 'Strange Brew', designed as a vehicle for Eric. By virtue of the fact that there wasn't enough material, they had to record things like 'Sunshine' which then became the biggest-selling single that Atlantic ever had! I remember people like Otis Redding and Booker T encouraging me. They loved that riff. I knew that it was a very commercial, world-beating riff that would catch on, but it was very difficult at the time to get the belief from Ahmet in particular. All that was going on behind the scenes."

The feeling began to grow among the band that there was a hidden agenda to elevate Clapton's role. "Stigwood and Eric too, were trying to make Eric into the star, with us as the backing people," says Bruce.

"Unfortunately, Eric just couldn't come up with the material. Even the stuff that he did write, he couldn't sing, like 'Tales Of Brave Ulysses'. He didn't have the confidence or power in his voice at that time to do something like that."

But back in the summer of '66, as far as their fans were concerned, Cream was a triumvirate, with equal gifts and powers. It was the whole point of the original concept, even if this apparently fell on deaf ears. On October 7th the debut single, 'Wrapping Paper' backed with 'Cat's Squirrel' was finally released on Stigwood's Reaction label.

The first product by the songwriting team of Jack Bruce and Pete Brown, it seemed almost deliberately designed to foil all preconceptions about the band and its direction. It had hardly any discernible guitar playing and the low key performance caused confusion among their fans.

"New Cream single too weird for us," was the comment in the MM's gossip column The Raver. A rather scathing anonymous review also took the band to task:

"Surprise, surprise! Their recording debut sees The Cream in a new light and one which will astound their fans, possibly even drive them to suicide. Jack Bruce takes the vocals on this Loving Spoonful-tinged Roaring Twenties number. Most disappointing is the musical content of the number which is nil. It has obvious commerciality and might even be a huge hit, but in the group's attempt at ultra-hipness and shock treatment, they may have outsmarted themselves. Music lovers should listen to the B-side 'Cat's Squirrel' a feedback fiery blues, spearheaded by Clapton and supercharged by Bruce and Baker."

It was claimed that some 10,000 copies of the single were withdrawn due to "pressing faults". 'Wrapping Paper' struggled to reach Number 24 in the charts in November. It was not an auspicious start. Although getting a hit single was important in terms of winning wider recognition, for most of their fans, live gigs were more relevant. It was wonderful to be able to walk into a small club and watch the three best young musicians of the day play exciting, rootsy innovative sounds while the sweat poured off the walls and the beer flowed at three shillings a pint. Cream presented an exhilarating spectacle in an age when most so-called 'beat groups' were pretty tame. And there was nothing predictable about their early performances. You couldn't even be sure if they would 'turn on' in the jazz sense of creating inspired moments of interplay and spontaneous improvisation.

The fact that it didn't always work made the good moments even greater. Rumours swept the corridors of rock power that some of their first gigs weren't particularly good. But that was often the case with the most celebrated bands of the period. I can remember seeing some Who performances at obscure venues that were incredibly lame and best forgotten. They made up for these disasters by playing with renewed fervour and brilliance elsewhere.

I missed Cream's first club gig at Cooks Ferry Inn but reports said they opened up with 'Hey Lawdie Mama' followed by 'The First Time I Met The Blues' and 'Traintime'. One eye-witness told how: "Enthusiastic shouting and cheering was reserved for the second half of their act, when they dropped their nerves and reduced the gap between numbers. Although Cream are still in the experimental stage, they are striving for perfection which, when it does come, will be little short of sensational."

I went to see Cream play at Klooks Kleek, a regular venue organised by the cheery promoter Dick Jordan at the Station Hotel, a pub in West Hampstead. It was on November 15, 1966 and the gig was part of a whole series of UK club dates.

As I parked my car and strode towards the pub, I was surprised to see Eric and Jack lurching somewhat furtively up the road towards me, sharing a joint. It seemed strange to see these celebrities casually wandering abroad just before a gig. Even in the laid-back Sixties, you somehow expected them to be whisked onto the premises by Rolls Royce, with a fleet of minders in tow. Perhaps Stigwood had the limo, while the boys were expected to arrive on foot. As a roving reporter I often found abandoned groups in urgent need of transport. I once drove The Who back from a gig at The Manor House to the West End, when they were left stranded with Keith Moon pilled-up and in a state of collapse. I also rescued Rod Stewart from a night club when he couldn't afford a cab home, and spirited Mick Jagger away from the Royal Festival Hall; when he was besieged by admirers. On another memorable occasion I packed eleven people in the car, most of whom were tripping on acid, including most of The Nice and a sizeable chunk of the audience from the Jazz & Blues Festival. We managed to get past a police cordon when I shouted: "Let us through – we're the Teenagers Of The Year". They thought we were the winners of a national newspaper competition. (Sadly the Ford's engine seized up in Soho Square and the Consul was crushed flat in front of my eyes by the hydraulic arm of the salvage truck.)

SHOCK TACTICS

However, on this occasion I didn't have to get Eric and Jack past any police blocks. We simply stumbled up the stairs and found the audience waiting for – what was the band called tonight? – oh yeah – "Ladies and gentlemen – CREAM!"

In the carpeted lounge where a succession of the greatest groups of the Sixties had performed, from Zoot Moneys Big Roll Band to Fleetwood Mac, it was possible to stand only feet away from the musicians who would later become venerated and idolised. But in 1966, this was 'the underground', a scene known only to an in-crowd of switched on fans and 'aware' music biz folk. Such gigs were more fun, and more satisfying for all concerned, than any mega stadium event.

It seemed to me that any doubts about Cream's ability to perform as a group and not just three star soloists were dispelled.

"One of their main strengths is their fantastic empathy," I wrote in my subsequent review. Yes, there'd been reports filtering back of 'bad performances' by Cream elsewhere on the tour, but it was good to see them obviously enjoying each other's playing. "They worked together like a team of bomb disposal experts and Eric Clapton played one of the most astounding solos of his career on 'Steppin' Out' which he sustained for minutes on end. Here is one of the most musically rewarding and fascinating groups making it today and if anybody should record a 'live' LP, it's The Cream."

Wise words, mate.

Meanwhile their chart entry with 'Wrapping Paper' at least ensured that the band maintained media interest, and they gave a succession of interviews. Jack Bruce told one reporter: "I must admit we wanted to shock people. We knew what everyone expected us to release. If only people weren't so prejudiced. Why can't they accept something for what it is – not what it was, or used to be like. Let's face it, it's damned easy for Eric Clapton to play blues. I can't tell you what I think of Clapton, he's probably the greatest blues guitarist in the world. It flows out of him. So it's easy for him to play blues, but far more difficult to go out and find his own music." Bruce emphasised that fact that they wanted Cream to establish its own style and create its own music.

"This is what we're out to do, and I think we're succeeding. Personally I think I can go no further than Cream, and I've worked with a lot of musicians."

During November, Stigwood flew to America to set up their first tour there, and during December the band went to Germany for TV shows and a brace of concerts throughout Europe.

The strain soon began to tell. Ginger Baker collapsed on stage at both Sussex University and at the Birdcage Club in Portsmouth and Jack Bruce also fell ill, which delayed the first album, intended for October release.

"I must admit we wanted to shock people. We knew what everyone expected us to release. If only people weren't so prejudiced. Why can't they accept something for what it is – not what it was, or used to be like."

In the midst of all this hard work, and just as Cream were beginning to establish themselves and make waves, there came a most unexpected rival. A brilliant young black American guitarist arrived in London and set up his own trio with a pair of English backing musicians. The guitarist could play the blues with infinite power and intensity and had an innovative style that threatened to blow rings around the best local players, including Pete Townshend, Jeff Beck and Eric Clapton. The newcomer was Jimi Hendrix with his band The Experience. In the event, both bands would prove to be able to function side by side, without loss of power or influence. Jimi and Eric would form a mutual admiration society and became firm friends. But there was no doubt that Hendrix, with his dynamic stage presence and powerful personality, was a major competitor.

In one of his earliest interviews Jimi said: "I played with Cream a week after getting to London. I think the one I like the best is Eric Clapton. I don't know too much about the other guys. Possibly Eric and I think along the same lines but it's hard to get it across to the other musicians and the other fifty million people who might be listening. I'm not sure if Eric is playing exactly what he wants to – but I know that if I just played my own scene all night, I'd probably bore everybody to death."

102

Doubtless Eric had been confiding in Hendrix and telling him he still had reservations about his role in Cream though outwardly Clapton was still indicating that he was happy and more fulfilled than he had been in The Yardbirds or The Bluesbreakers.
He told MM's Nick Jones that he had changed his mind about a few things, including his plan to leave the country to become recognised.

"I was a loner when I said America was the only place I would get anywhere. I was out on my own at the time. Now I'm in with a band I really dig and I don't want to go to America other than just to see the place and find out what's happening. I'm only concerned with Cream at the moment. Certainly my whole musical outlook has changed. I listen to the same records but with a different ear. Before I'd always listen from a guitarist's point of view. More is expected of me in Cream but I don't believe I've ever played so well in my life. I know that a lot of biased listeners say that all we are playing is pop. In actual fact, closer listening reveals that none of us are playing anything that vaguely resembles pop. I don't think our record 'Wrapping Paper' is too weird. It's a very good tune and very commercial with the sort of feel that represents us."

Eric was strangely pessimistic about the possibility of mass acceptance for Cream however: "I don't believe we'll ever get over to them. People will always listen with biased ears, look through unbelieving eyes and with preconceived ideas. The only way to combat this is to present them with as many facets of your music as possible. Some people will come to see Ginger or hear Jack's singing, or look at the clothes you wear. Therefore we've got to please them all. Do everybody in!"

Eric agreed that he had changed during the past half year. "Jack Bruce has had a tremendous influence on my playing and my personality. It's a lot easier to play in a blues band than in a group where you've got to play purely your own individual ideas. You have got to put over a completely new kind of music. Jack, Ginger and I have absorbed a lot of music."

Amidst the onrush of gigs, TV appearances and interviews, the band were expected to come up with more material for a new single and their debut album. Eric hadn't developed as a writer, Ginger Baker tried his hand without great success, which left Jack Bruce to come up with the new songs. But even Jack couldn't do it all on his own, and an ally was brought into the camp; poet and wordsmith Pete Brown.

'Wrapping Paper' had been credited to Bruce and Brown, much to Baker's chagrin who thought he had contributed to its creation in the studio. It became a bone of contention when it was realised that Bruce/Brown might earn more money than Clapton or Baker from publishing royalties. But as Jack always contended, it was only because he came to the sessions armed with material. The band had little choice than to accept what he had to offer. In any case, the bassist was responsible for some of their greatest hits, including 'I Feel Free' coupled with Jack's composition 'N.S.U.' their second single, released in December, 1966. The record soared to Number 11 in the charts in February. 'I Feel Free' featured Eric using his new sustained 'woman tone' sound which he obtained by altering the bass, treble and volume controls on his trusty Gibson.

> *"This is what we're out to do, and I think we're succeeding. Personally I think I can go no further than Cream, and I've worked with a lot of musicians."*

Now they had a palpable hit, the band was invited to appear on BBC TV's Top Of The Pops. They dressed up in prison garb for the occasion.

Accompanying the release of 'I Feel Free' was the band's eagerly-awaited debut album 'Fresh Cream' (Reaction). It was produced by Robert Stigwood and recorded in a tiny studio in a few hours. Eric would reminisce years later that they had no real idea how to make a record: "We were just having fun, like kids really."

Each song was run through a couple of times before they went for a 'take'. In this way they put down performances that might have been technically more proficient but were at least spontaneous and honest.

The tracks included 'N.S.U.', 'Sleepy Time', 'Dreaming' Sweet Wine', 'Spoonful', 'Cat's Squirrel', 'Four Until Late', 'Rollin' and Tumblin'', 'I'm So Glad' and Baker's drum solo 'Toad'.

Reviews were generally good, although some critics suggested that the material was already out of date and expected "more sensational things to come".

The material was split fairly evenly between their exciting treatment of traditional blues like Willie Dixon's 'Spoonful' and Muddy Water's 'Rollin' And Tumblin'' and original material. Ginger Baker and Jack's wife Janet co-wrote 'Sweet Wine' but despite grumbles about the dominance of the Bruce/Brown partnership, there weren't many examples of their work together on the first album. They would be become more apparent on the band's second, 'Disraeli Gears'.

Bruce was proud of his contribution but felt he had to defend accusations of dominance. He recalled that right from the start they had a limited repertoire. "Nobody had written any songs specifically for the group. I had a few songs that turned out to be absolutely wrong, so we started out with standard blues. After we gigged around, we got more of a repertoire together and dropped some of the numbers that obviously weren't right and wrote some more. The reason for my dominance is that nobody was writing enough apart from me. I was writing lots of songs. When we went to do 'Disraeli Gears', for instance, the idea was that everybody would write an equal number of songs and we'd record them all and take the best ones. But we turned up to the session and I had about ten songs, Ginger had two songs and Eric had one. We had five days to make an album. There was no time to do anything else.

"I regretted that at the time, 'cos I wanted to play their music as much as my own. We were on the road for months and then we'd have five days to write an album. Everybody would write songs, but when it came to it, nobody had any except me. The drag is that if Eric had written more, it would have been incredible. 'I Feel Free' was my first attempt to write a pop single and do something in three minutes. That was very much influenced by The Beatles, who were doing those fabulous singles. It was a bit controversial because of the beginning, which started off with acapella vocals. I was always doing it to them! Eric saw the potential of that song but he was very upset by his playing on it and I remember us having a big fight because he wanted to re-record it, which would have been quite difficult. It was done in London on a four track machine and it had fairly intricate backing vocals. To try and get that down on four tracks was quite hard and we didn't have the necessary knowledge. We didn't have somebody like George Martin to help us. We were in at the deep end and none of us had much experience in the studio. I'd only done a few sessions and in those days musicians were like the workers who weren't even allowed into the control room. We were very inexperienced. The first recordings that we did, both 'Fresh Cream' and the singles, were done in such a rush that I was amazed they came out as well as they did."

"'Wrapping Paper' was considered to be a bit 'off the wall.' But then it was my idea to do something like that. Everybody thought we'd do some storming blues thing. In fact it is a 12-bar blues. But my idea was to keep people guessing and never do what they expect. Although it wasn't a huge hit, it did make an impression. I remember us doing Ready, Steady Go! (ITV) with that song. I remember playing bowed bass."

'Fresh Cream' got to Number Six in the UK album charts and even got into the Top Forty in the States, which helped pave the way for their first visit there in March. The band were still playing at village halls and pubs in England, but they were on the verge of an American breakthrough. Ginger Baker would soon be able to swop his Rover car for a rather more expensive Jensen Intercepter, Eric would ultimately swop his succession of flats for a Surrey mansion and Jack Bruce could even afford to buy his own Scottish island. But they still had a lot more hard work ahead of them.

Chapter Five
ROCK AND POETRY

With a Little Help From My Friends' was one of the more poignant and touching Beatles songs that charmed the populace during 1967. It seemed to summarise everyone's efforts to get on with their lives amidst the frantic, pressurised pop boom. Sung by Ringo Starr on 'Sgt Pepper's Lonely Hearts Club Band' and later covered to dramatic effect by Joe Cocker, the sentiments could be applied to a variety of situations.

Certainly Cream, in its urgent quest for material, needed more than a little help. And the most important friend to come to their aid was Pete Brown; poet, percussionist, and anarchist, who co-wrote many of their greatest hits.

Brown had got to know Baker and Bruce mainly through their colleagues, Dick Heckstall-Smith and Graham Bond. They all had past associations with Brown's first love, the jazz and poetry movement. This had flowered in the early Sixties, when poetry readings were given alongside jazz instrumental accompaniment. It was an interesting idea and one of the first examples of 'mixed media'.

When Cream urgently needed lyrics for their debut single 'Wrapping Paper', Ginger called in Pete Brown. It would be the start of Brown's productive association with the fledgling supergroup, one that would bring the poverty-stricken poet unexpected financial rewards.

Not content with being Cream's lyricist, Pete also developed his own career as a singer and band leader, and ran such groups as The Battered Ornaments and Piblokto. He later had a band with Graham Bond, billed as Bond and Brown and more recently he has toured with his partner Phil Ryan in a group called Interociter. Says Brown: "I was the world's worst singer for many years! I started singing well after a lot of work and a lot of lessons. I went on the road as a professional singer for ten years from 1968 onwards."

Brown lives in a large Victorian house, high on the hills of north London that over look the Arsenal football ground. Once a dabbler in drink and drugs, Pete forswore rock's worst vices just at the point when many of his contemporaries were starting to take the plunge into the hard stuff. He wears open-toed sandals and still holds dear the beliefs and values of the Sixties.

When he was a young beatnik, at the forefront of London's underground scene, he suddenly found himself propelled into the capitalistic world of pop success. He had been earning twenty pounds a week as an itinerant verse reader. Then he made the traumatic transition into the big time. Brown earned forty thousand a year in royalties from the songs he co-wrote for Cream. It was exciting and confusing and he now freely admits that he didn't know what to do with all the money.

When he first heard about the plan to form Cream, he had been leading a haphazard self-destructive lifestyle. "It was a funny time for me because I was in the last throes of my drugs and boozing period, which I stopped in 1967. In fact 1966 was a kind of horrible climax to it all."

It's a cliché to say that if you remember the Sixties, you weren't really there, but Pete admits that many of his memories of Cream are either blurred or erased from his consciousness. Yet he has total recall of the day when Baker and Bruce broached him about the project.

"They called me from a studio in Chalk Farm. Jack and Ginger said they'd done a song and needed some words."
Brown had been making a living from reading poetry, "and being a bum!" He and partner Mike Horowitz had a residency at the Marquee Club that they shared with Alexis Korner's Blues Incorporated. Pete used to hang out with the musicians and would occasionally team-up with them on stage.

"Graham Bond and Dick Heckstall-Smith had already done a few gigs with us back in 1963. Before that, in 1961 there had been a Big Band Jazz & Poetry concert at St Pancras Town Hall and they were all on that except for Jack. So we were all kind of connected."

Brown shared a flat with Bruce for a while and they had a mutual friend in jazz trombonist John Mumford.

"Jack and Dick and various others all lived in a place in Miranda Road, a house near Archway, owned by a sculptor," recalls Pete. "The local kids scrawled a big sign in the road saying 'BETNICKS' with an arrow pointing towards the house. It was in the early days of the beatniks."

Despite their rather alarming proto-hippy appearance, which so disturbed the neighbours, Pete doesn't think Jack led a particularly wild life. He was already married to Janet and was quite settled, serious and hard-working.

"Jack had married very young, and wasn't being that crazy. But I was living a wild life and trying to find whatever bits of myself that were relevant, and trying to destroy quite a lot of other bits!"

The major event in the lives of this loose association of musicians, artists and writers was the formation of The Graham Bond Organisation in 1964. Says Brown: "I used to go to as many of their gigs as possible because I was a big fan of the band. I loved it. I still think it was one of the greatest bands Britain has ever produced. So I was around them quite a lot, and when Jack and Ginger left the Organisation, Graham wanted me to write for it. But that was after I had already started doing stuff for Cream. They had called me and asked if I could come down and start work straight away."

111

It seemed strange that the band didn't feel confident about writing their own lyrics and, says Pete: "Well that was the funny thing y'know. Jack and Ginger were both extremely intelligent people and I didn't know Eric that well. I only knew him slightly through people like Ben Palmer, who was a road manager and musician. He had been with Eric in The Glands on that funny tour to Greece. I never really understood why they wanted me to write for them. I suppose they wanted something a bit different and sophisticated and I was a kind of happening poet at the time. Not that I was earning any money! I had a reputation and I loved music. In retrospect, it was fairly sensible because Cream's touring schedule was so tight that there really wasn't time for them to write anyway. That's the reason why Jack and I came up with most of the stuff. The others needed more time to think and get it together."

Brown was used to writing fast from his poetry reading days, when he had to vary his material from night to night.
"We were writing new stuff every time we performed anywhere. It was also an amphetamine-driven thing for me at the time and I was trying, probably not very successfully, to improvise poetry quite a lot. The amphetamines speeded me up, but I wouldn't recommend it to anybody because it does a lot of bad things. At the time nobody knew that, during the first flush of the drug culture. I really liked the idea of staying up for three or four days and it being night all the time. That's what 'speed' did for you."

Brown's prolific output ensured that a high percentage of his material was used by Cream. He worked with both Ginger and Eric and emphasises that all the band were capable of bringing in songs. However, the sudden success of the band, and the realisation that Brown was getting a large share of the royalties, put a strain on the relationship, at least as far as the founder member of the band was concerned.

"They all wrote their own stuff and Jack did things like 'N.S.U.' which was really good. But it took them a while to get those things together. I was writing all the time and capable of providing ideas fast. Ginger had very far out ideas that were terrific. I remember a tune he got off a record of Polynesian music and we wrote some ideas to that. I don't think it was ever made into a demo. Ginger was a progressive jazzer by nature and probably still is. It was before he got into his main African influence. He was interested in world music when very few people were. Jack and Eric were into that too. All three were very broadminded about music. They weren't just listening to blues or being 'British jazz purists'."

On the first occasion that Brown worked with Cream, he went along to the studio and they played him a backing track for the song that became 'Wrapping Paper'. Pete had spent much of his childhood going to the movies, and had a penchant for cinematic images that expressed themselves in his lyrics. He feels now that he overloaded 'Wrapping Paper' with too many images for a debut song, but at least it gave Cream a start.

"I think it was helped into the chart by the management!" laughs Pete.

He understands that there was some dismay at the sort of material Cream put out as singles. Instead of rock, blues and lots of improvisation, fans got quirky pop songs and strange ditties – interesting in their way, but not always the kind of stuff designed to impress pipe-smoking, real ale drinkers at the Blues & Jive Appreciation Society.

Explains Pete: "Jack and I sat down and did all sorts of funny bits. What a lot of people don't realise is that all of our generation were entirely fuelled by two kinds of humour. Number one was obviously Black American jazz hip type humour, and the other thing was the British equivalent, which was The Goon Show."

Throughout the 1950s, British children as well as adults listened with wonder and joy to the weekly BBC Home Service comedy show. Starring Spike Milligan, Michael Bentine, Peter Sellers and Harry Secombe, it broke new ground in radio humour and blasted a refreshing note of anarchy throughout a rather stuffy post war decade. Only the Goons dared mimic Churchill and Parliamentary debates in the age before satire, Private Eye and Spitting Image. The Goons' humour appealed to the British en masse, from Prince Charles to John Lennon.

"The Goon Show was fantastically important," asserts Brown. "The surrealism and cynicism of The Goons pervade everything produced at that time, and is still with us. Certainly in those days it was all powerful and that's why Cream did funny lyrics as well. One of the lyrics we wrote had Jack singing: 'He started off in Canada selling fridges to the Eskimos...' It was the first version of 'Doing That Scrapyard Thing'. It was a surreal, biographical thing, because Jack lived in Canada for a while." Goonish humour spilled over from their lyrics into their whole outlook and it was behind Eric's early ideas for their proposed stage act.

"That's why the band wanted to have a stuffed bear on stage with them," says Brown. "There was a strong element of British humour. People thought it was going to be all hard-core blues and a direct follow on from John Mayall. Of course, there were many other elements which to some extent made it more successful and more interesting than what John Mayall was doing."

Clapton's desire to put stuffed animals on stage was only a whim, however. As Pete says: "They weren't being theatrical. Of course the real drama was obviously in the relationship. They didn't need any props. The conflict between Jack and Ginger had carried on over from the Bond Organisation. They are like brothers who compete. That's what they really are. It's like 'Hey, cop this... follow that you bastard'. It's quite funny and makes for very interesting music. It's probably harder to do it that way than for everybody to love each other, and say 'Let's get into a groove man'. They respect each other – of course they do – but it's a strange relationship. Ginger once said to me: 'I'm a black hearted bastard'. The thing is, we recently had a really nice conversation about ecology, because he is very concerned about the fate of the world, as Jack always was. I was quite surprised, as I was always wary of Ginger. We'd had a few unpleasant run-ins. But he was terribly nice and seems to have mellowed quite a lot. The thing is, if you have a big personality, then you are never the easiest person to get on with anyway, because you expand all over the place. There are always people telling you how great you are and hanging around."

"All three were very broadminded about music. They weren't just listening to blues or being 'British jazz purists'."

The abrasive tension that existed between Baker and Bruce helped sustain the tension within Cream's music and always ensured it was dynamic and competitive, but it didn't make life easy for the third member. For the rest of his musical career, Clapton would tend to employ musicians who were perhaps less inspired, but were easier to get on with.

"Both Jack and Ginger are driven men and they both believe in their own talent. You can't say it's because they come from working class backgrounds, because a lot of such people have no motivation at all. But they both believe they have something to say. They are supremely individual musicians who don't owe that much to anybody anymore," explains Brown.

Baker could be aggressive and suspicious, mainly due to his experiences of being ripped off, and Pete Brown found himself being regarded with hostility when it was realised he was earning as much as, if not more than, the man who had actually come up with the idea for the band, to wit, one G Baker, drummer of this parish.

"I had worked on some things with Ginger and then he would say 'Oh, I'm afraid I lost your lyric and I had to do something else'. Later on, when he was not being very pleasant, he virtually accused me of stealing his birthright by writing all those songs and copping a living from them. He perhaps felt he should have been doing it.

"On the other hand, with all due respect, I did help the main hits along quite a bit, which did quite a lot for them, and besides he didn't come up with as much stuff as I did."

"Both Jack and Ginger are driven men and they both believe in their own talent. You can't say it's because they come from working class backgrounds, because a lot of such people have no motivation at all. But they both believe they have something to say. They are supremely individual musicians who don't owe that much to anybody anymore."

In the words of Syd Barret and the I Ching, action leads on to fortune, and Pete certainly found his hard work paid off.
"I was overwhelmed with the whole business anyway. I went from earning twenty quid a week for doing poetry readings at the height of my fame as a poet, to earning forty grand a year as a songwriter, which in those days was a great deal of money. It was such an overwhelming thing for me, I didn't know what to do with it. I was living in Montagu Square in a nice flat. I used to get cabs round to Selfridges and keep them waiting for hours while I bought everything – ha ha! That didn't last very long but it was a strange period of time. 'I've got money – I don't understand this at all!' You see I'd been a bum. All I'd ever done before was sell shoes with my parents, when they used to take pity on me. I didn't like doing it anyway. I'd sooner hitch-hike to Liverpool to read poetry for ten shillings. The great thing about those times was that everyone was extremely broadminded. You could do anything."

PETE'S MADNESS

Despite the freedoms of the Swinging Sixties, there was a price to be paid for over-indulgence. "I must admit I was in a very peculiar state at the time when we were trying to write the first lot of things together," recalls Brown. "What happened was that I had gone into overload and had a very awful trip. I was spiked. It probably wasn't acid, it was more likely to have been DMT (a more powerful form of LSD), and as a result I got very peculiar and started to get anxiety attacks and the horrors. I'd had this trip when I was pissed and stoned. It acted like a kind of aversion therapy and after that whenever I picked up a glass of beer or smoked a joint I started to get real bad horrors and would have to rush out in the middle of a recording session. The band were tolerant but probably didn't quite understand what I was going through. I was just very peculiar and in the end I decided that I would knock the whole business on the head and I haven't had a drink or a drug since 1967."

Cream's second single 'I Feel Free' wasn't written with Brown's liberation from alcohol and drug abuse in mind.

"It came a bit before then. It was more of an amphetamine-fuelled piece of psychedelia. But I wasn't trying to push drugs through songs, unlike a lot of other people. All I was trying to do was use the imagery in my head that was based on watching millions of films. 'Wrapping Paper' was about two people who could only meet in a picture, in a deserted old house by the sea. It was just an image really. God knows what it had to do with the blues! It was not hugely successful but it was kind of provocative and made you think. Jack and I came from poetry and jazz backgrounds, and we built things to last. I had a strong feeling that pop music was somewhat abusive of people and I wanted them to have some good music and interesting words. Perhaps that was a bit idealistic, but it seemed to work. That was partly inspired by the fact there were some good things around at the time."

Brown credits Syd Barrett of Pink Floyd for having encouraged him to be more open and experimental with lyrics.

"Syd did quite a lot for me in terms of first of all being British, and actually finding a British voice. His 'Arnold Layne' had a certain influence on me because I found it liberating."

CR
Stran

"Here was a song with a nice, interesting tune that was about British weirdness, which I thought was tremendous. It was successful and got to people, and that was kind of inspiring. It enabled me to write things that weren't very trans-Atlantic. Funnily enough, I'm now writing blues material for black artists which is very strange."

Pete puts it down to being Jewish.

"I note that there is a tradition for Jewish people to write material for black artists, like Leiber & Stoller who are two of my idols. I figure I'm part of a tradition!"

To produce Cream material, Bruce and Brown would sit down and write songs together in spare moments between tours. Jack would play piano or rhythm guitar and work out the themes, while Brown supplied the lyrics.

After 'I Feel Free' came a spate of recordings that produced what is now known as 'the famous lost demo session'. This included such compositions as 'Clear Out' and 'Weird Of Hermiston', and another song called 'Look Now Princess' which surfaced on a recent Jack Bruce album.

Explains Brown: "There were five or six numbers, the demos of which mysteriously vanished. They were actually demo'd by Cream and Robert Stigwood may have thought they were going in the wrong direction and were not commercial and sort of suppressed them. I'm not sure if that's true but they mysteriously vanished then turned up again about five years ago. We re-wrote 'Princess' and put it on a Jack Bruce album, called 'A Question Of Time'. It may have been a bootleg, because everything gets bootlegged!"

One of Brown's most famous Cream co-compositions 'White Room' is frequently played by Clapton today. "That was based on an eight page poem that ended up as a one page song. That was the only one that was really about me. I didn't live anywhere for a while, then I got some money and moved into this tiny white room. It was a real place – right next door to a fire station as well, so the alarms would keep going off. That was where I had the nasty trip and that's where I finally stopped boozing and drugging. It was a kind of landmark situation, and a new start for me. Then we did all kinds of things like 'Take It Back', which is sort of about the draft and Vietnam."

"There were blues into pop things, like 'Sunshine Of Your Love', which I wrote some of and has become an anthem. I'm not too happy about 'Sunshine' – I wrote two thirds of the lyrics and Eric wrote the hook line. That song has paid for lots of my life. Along with 'White Room' and 'I Feel Free' those songs have been huge and continual earners."

Brown didn't have a contract with Cream and says: "I was very wise. I just did it on a song by song basis and never had an exclusive contract with that organisation. I believe Cream received a very small percentage of their earnings. Cream was among the highest earning acts in the world at that time. They got $68,000 at one gig alone on their last tour, but what happened to it all nobody knows. They didn't get it in their pockets."

In the race to get Cream established, there were very few opportunities for the whole band to sit down and write together. Says Brown: "Nowadays if you say, 'I will not tour until I have written all the songs for the album', that's fine. But in those days they were out on the road. Nobody ever believed they would sell the amount of records they did, so that was another mistaken strategy. Nobody ever believed that you should spend vast amounts of time in the studio, like Fleetwood Mac, who would later spend two years making an album. But they weren't such a great live band. They weren't so exciting and weren't such good musicians. Cream needed to go out and play. When it came to composing stuff they could have done with more time."
Pete Brown never went on the road with Cream. "During the period of time when I was freaked out, loud music used to frighten me, so I used to find it hard to go and listen to them. I went to one nice gig at a May Ball in Oxford that was very funny. There were all sorts of great incidents. Jack Bruce found a big old fashioned coal scuttle, full of puke. He put it in one of the don's rooms."

He also remembers Ginger Baker being offered something to eat and the drummer wolfing down 'about half a ton of food'. Ginger also cycled his bike through the bar causing a great commotion. The band were playing in a marquee set up in the college grounds, and not many people even bothered to listen to them. "They played some of the songs they actually hadn't played live very much, like 'Dance The Night Away' (from 'Disraeli Gears')," recalls Pete. "Usually they got into blues jams and didn't always do the more difficult songs, which sometimes would have needed more instrumentation to make them successful."

"They always talked about getting more instruments, which they say was one of the reasons why they broke up. They wanted more people in there to take the pressure away from the three of them, who were getting claustrophobic. Also each one of them had to fulfil the function of two players."

It was curious how Cream developed in fits and starts. Even when 'I Feel Free' was racing up the charts, the band were still playing small venues, like the Ram Jam Club, a pub in the back streets of Brixton, where they appeared on January 29th, 1967. Eventually they were given a more prestigious spot when they were presented at London's Saville Theatre. It was the first time many of their fans could actually sit down and watch the band in comfort.

The Beatles' manager Brian Epstein had taken over the theatre in Shaftesbury Avenue for regular Sunday night concerts. The Bee Gees, The Who, Bonzo Dog Doo Dah Band, Lee Dorsey, Fats Domino and many more starred in shows at the plush but intimate venue, creating nights which live on in the memory of all who were fortunate enough to attend them. Under The Beatles patronage, they seemed like rock's own royal command performances. The night that Epstein died from a drug overdose on August 27, Jimi Hendrix was playing at The Saville. His second show was cancelled as a mark of respect. Today the building is a cinema but whenever I pass it, I remember the angry girl standing on the steps of the foyer shouting furiously as news of the tragedy and cancellation spread: "Who's Brian Epstein!"

Cream played there in February and, inspired perhaps by the setting and the VIP guests, they gave a thrilling performance. In my eyewitness account I gave special praise to Baker's drumming. I was anxious not to set one member of the band up against the others, but there was no doubt Ginger was on top form that night.

I wrote: "Ginger Baker played one of the finest solos of his career at The Saville on Sunday. His solo 'Toad' was a masterpiece of drum solo construction. It had pace, direction and built to a fantastic climax. He showed complete control of his seven-drum kit. Eric Clapton, too, played brilliantly, especially on 'Steppin' Out' and 'I'm So Glad', which suddenly turned into the '1812 Overture'."

Programme cover from Saville Theatre, Shaftesbury Avenue

Ginger's spectacular solo, which he had been building up in layers of ideas since his earliest days with Alexis Korner and Graham Bond, would prove exciting for audiences who had never heard a rock band drummer like him. He wasn't a perfectionist, and nor was his playing facile. It was an emotional outburst of temperament, a physical expression of a human need for fulfilment. Sometimes Ginger made mistakes, dropped a stick or seemed to be struggling to find a way round a mental block to his progress. It was the sight of his ultimate victory over a drum kit that made audiences want to cheer, just as they would cheer an athlete struggling to win a marathon. Indeed Ginger told me: 'I think the way I play, as well as being musical, is very athletic. I use all my limbs. I get near to a blackout every night after the solo and sometimes I can't stand up. I play the solo to a pattern so that the others know when to come in, but I try to do something new every time. I never play the same solo twice, but if you're playing with a band, you've got to play to a pattern. I like to get excited by the drums before I play the climax."

> *"They always talked about getting more instruments, which they say was one of the reasons why they broke up."*

Although Ginger had a reputation for being bad-tempered and violent, he disputed that he enjoyed being involved in fights. 'I'm not interested," he insisted. "I've been in some but I do everything in my power to get out. I'm a pacifist. He who strikes first loses an argument. That's an old Chinese proverb. I've lost a few arguments. I've got an Irish temper which has taken years to get under control. I'd rather kick a door in than somebody's head. Then it only hurts me. I've kicked my drums over and thrown them downstairs many times! I'm pretty easy-going most of the time. I just don't like being late for a gig. I get in a state and start panicking."

During February the band made a short film of 'I Feel Free' – an early example of a 'pop promo'. Curiously, this ran into problems in America, where it was supposedly banned as it showed the band dressed as monks. "The Americans felt it might offend people's religious susceptibilities," said the band's management. It was probably more likely that TV networks wouldn't show it because they'd never heard of Cream. There was nothing like a good 'banning' to get news coverage, as Jimi Hendrix' management discovered.

GEARING UP FOR AMERICA

In March, the band went to Scandinavia for a short tour and played in Copenhagen (6), Stockholm (7) and Gothenburg (8), and then set off for the land of opportunity. They arrived in America on March 25. 1967. Cream were booked to play for a week on the Murray The K Easter Show at New York's RKO Theatre, in Manhattan. Smokey Robinson And The Miracles were supposed to top the bill and the band had only a brief spot to get their music across. Murray The K was a top DJ on New York's Radio WINS who had helped to introduce America to The Beatles and The Stones. The idea of his 'Music In The Fifth Dimension' stage show was to present as many acts as possible within an hour, and then change over the teenage audience. The shows started at 10am each day and went on until midnight.

Among the acts expected to play under these bizarre conditions were Simon & Garfunkel, The Who, Mitch Ryder, Wilson Pickett and The Lovin' Spoonful. There was only about five minutes for each act and Cream found themselves playing 'I Feel Free' and 'I'm So Glad' six times a day for ten days, using borrowed equipment. In the event, most of the time the theatre was half empty and Cream didn't go down as well as The Who. Chaos reigned as the show overran each day.

Ginger Baker described the affair as a classic example of how not to promote a rock band. Clapton and Townshend coped with this madness in time-honoured fashion by engaging in a cream cake battle backstage which culminated in the dressing room showers overflowing. Murray The K was driven to distraction and the show was abandoned, losing some $27,000.

Jack Bruce remembers their American experience with mixed feelings. "I think that was another management mistake. We did interminable tours there. One went on for seven months before we finally made it. It obviously helped to break the band, but it also broke the band up. When you do seven months of one nighters – you really feel the strain. The first thing we did – The Murray The K show with The Who – was fairly chaotic. We did four or five shows a day at the RKO Theatre, which didn't do us much good. I think we got cut down to half a song towards the end!"

Despite everything the band enjoyed getting know New York and Eric told me about their fun and games on his return to London. He thought the Murray The K show was hilarious. "It was great – too much! The audience were mostly 13 to 14-year-old teeny boppers. Everybody went down well and as we only had one or two numbers each, everybody pulled the stops out. The Who stole the show. They only had to smash everything up and everybody was on their feet. We did 'I'm So Glad' and 'I Feel Free' but the whole thing had nothing to do with music."

Eric told me how much they had enjoyed visiting Greenwich Village: "It was like the English Musical Appreciation Society. I sat in with a couple of the Mothers Of Invention and Mitch Ryder at the Cafe Au Go Go where Jimi Hendrix used to play. I made a lot of friends there, including Al Cooper who used to be the organist on a lot of Dylan's tracks. We took the actual show as a joke. There was no chance for Ginger to play his solo and we had to use The Who's equipment because we couldn't take any with us and there was none provided – as usual."
Eric explained that Wilson Pickett and Mitch Ryder topped the bill and Smokey Robinson dropped out. "He refused to do it because it wasn't his scene."

"I think that was another management mistake. We did interminable tours there. One went on for seven months before we finally made it. It obviously helped to break the band, but it also broke the band up."

"New York is incredible, I'd love to live there. Everybody is so much more hip to the music scene – taxi drivers talking about James Brown. Can you imagine that in London?"
Eric loved the Village and was amazed to discover that the shops stayed open all night. He saw the Mothers Of Invention and hailed them as one of the best bands in America. "They don't take that LP they made seriously. They are really sending up the psychedelic scene. Jack and Ginger enjoyed themselves. Ginger had never been to a foreign country before where they spoke English and they could understand him, so he kept very quiet, placid and kind."

I asked Eric about the battle at the RKO corral.

"Well we had all these 14 pound bags of flour and eggs that we were going to use on stage on the last night, but Murray got to hear about it and said we wouldn't get paid if we did, so we spread them all around the dressing rooms. The whole cast joined in and Pete Townshend ended up swimming around in his dressing room, fully clothed, in a foot of water when his shower overflowed! It was rumoured that Murray spent $30,000 on the show and lost $27,000. He was very distraught, wandering about throwing his hands up in the air. He hadn't bargained for the casual English approach and he expected us to be leaping around, doing a James Brown thing. It just wasn't our kind of show."

Jack Bruce thought the gig at The Cafe Au Go Go made the band in New York.

"We had Buffalo Springfield opening up for us, and we got a cult following. At the same time we also did The Village Theatre which became The Fillmore East. It was an old Jewish Vaudeville Theatre and we were one of the first people in when it became a rock venue. The promoter Bill Graham was very important to the band. He saw the potential of Cream and when we went to San Francisco later in the year, he put us on for ten days at The Fillmore West. We played with The Electric Flag and Gary Burton. Bill Graham was great. He'd put a jazz, blues and rock band all on the same bill." (Tragically Bill Graham died in a helicopter crash in 1993).

Although the band couldn't see the point of playing US pop package shows, Pete Brown, back in England, believed it was a useful experience.

"After all, they were playing in the UK to a slightly larger version of the same audience they had played to with Graham Bond and John Mayall. They got packed houses, but they were still only playing clubs. Cream wasn't just a blues band. It was also a band that was going into areas parallel with things that Jimi Hendrix was doing. Hendrix was playing in the psychedelic clubs, and they weren't."

"Stigwood wouldn't let them play places like Middle Earth, (London's hippy club in Covent Garden). People think of Cream as a psychedelic band, but they never played hippy venues until they went to the States. I used to tell them they should play Middle Earth, because that crowd would have absolutely loved them."

DISRAELI GEARS

Towards the end of their first US trip Cream managed to fit in time to record their second album. They were sent to the Atlantic studios in New York and teamed up with American producer Felix Pappalardi, who was also a respected arranger and musician.

'Fresh Cream' had been produced by Robert Stigwood but the band weren't entirely happy with his expertise in such matters. Pappalardi was brought in to work alongside engineer Tom Dowd. The title of the subsequent block-busting album stemmed from a conversation the band were having about racing bicycles. Ginger was an expert in such matters, and he cracked up when he heard one of the roadies refer to 'Disraeli gears' when he actually meant 'derailleur gears'. At any rate 'Disraeli Gears' was a much better title than the original, which was going to be plain old 'Cream'.

The material on the second album avoided direct cover versions of blues standards, and featured much more of Pete Brown's lyrics as well as the first contributions from Clapton.
"If you listen to the difference between the first album and the second record it was a giant leap. The guys will acknowledge that," says Pete Brown. "They will say that Felix was the right producer for Cream. He knew what to do and made it a success for the American public and, through them, for the rest of the world. Stigwood wasn't a producer. There was this horrible idea around then that managers could produce. They wanted their hands on everything, and people were greedy. One of the reasons people were greedy was because of the dreaded British music business syndrome.

"Jack Bruce began to realise what was going down in the studio and he created something that was so difficult for Stigwood to understand that it was actually hard to fuck up!"

The philosophy was: 'This is going to be finished in a year, we've got to milk it dry, and then drop it'. That still goes on to some extent."

TOM JONES

Recording Vocalist

1. **TOM JONES**
2. **CLIFF RICHARD**
3. **JOHN LENNON**
4. Stevie Winwood
5. Jack Bruce
6. Scott Walker
7. Gary Brooker
8. Lulu
9. Engelbert Humperdinck
10. Eric Burdon
11. Donovan
12. Jimi Hendrix
13. Cat Stevens
14. Georgie Fame
15. Paul Jones
16. John Mayall
17. Chris Farlowe
18. Ray Davies
19. Steve Marriott
20. Jess Roden
    Arthur Brown
    Roger Daltry

BEAT INSTRUMEN
1967 GOL
STAR AW

Lead Guitarist

1. **ERIC CLAPTON**
2. **JIMI HENDRIX**
3. **HANK MARVIN**
4. Jeff Beck
5. Peter Green
6. George Harrison
7. Pete Townshend
8. Alvin Lee
9. Tony Hicks
10. Roy Wood
11. Steve Marriott
12. Albert Lee
13. Mick Taylor
14. Syd Barrett
15. Dave Mason
    Martin Stone

Bass Guitarist

1. **JACK BRUCE**
2. **NOEL REDDING**
3. **PAUL McCARTNEY**
4. John Rostill
5. John Macvie
6. John Entwhistle
7. Bern Calvert
8. Bill Wyman
9. Tab Martin
10. Plonk Lane
11. Pete Quaife
12. Roger Walters
13. Jet Harris
14. Eric Haydock
15. Maurice Gibb
    Klaus Voorman
    Ace Kefford

Drummer

1. **GINGER BAKER**
2. **KEITH MOON**
3. **BRIAN BENNETT**
4. Mitch Mitchell
5. Bobby Elliott
6. Ainsley Dunbar
7. Trevor Morais
8. Ringo Starr
9. Jon Hiseman
10. Keef Hartley
11. Andrew Steele
12. Bev Bevan
13. Blinky Davidson
14. Kenny Clare
15. Mick Avory
16. Tony Newman
    Charlie Watts

Keyboard Playe

1. **ALAN PRICE**
2. **STEVIE WINWO**
3. **GEORGIE FAME**
4. Brian Auger
5. Matthew Fisher
6. Gary Brooker
7. Manfred Mann
8. Graham Bond
9. Alan Haven
10. Ian McLagan
11. John Mayall
12. Keith Emmerson
    Roy Phillips
14. Wynder K. Frog
15. Dudley Moore
    Zoot Money

ERIC CLAPTON

JACK BRUCE

GINGER BAKER

ALAN PRICE

20

134

JIMI HENDRIX EXPERIENCE

Recording Manager

1. GEORGE MARTIN
2. MICKY MOST
3. DENNY CORDELL
4. Norrie Paramour
5. Mike Vernon
6. Chas Chandler
7. Kit Lambert
8. Andrew Oldham
9. Shel Talmy
10. Robert Stigwood
11. Mike Hurst
12. Jimmy Millar
    Mark Wirtz
14. Steve Rowland
15. Tony Hatch

Best Group on Stage

1. JIMI HENDRIX EX-
   PERIENCE
2. THE WHO
3. THE CREA
4. The Shadow
5. The Hollies
6. The Move
7. Traffic
8. John Ma
   breaker
9. Geno V
   Ram J

10. Pink Floyd
11. The Small Faces
12. Dave Dee and Co. Ltd.
    The Bee Gees
    Alan Bown!
    oes
    b Band

ass & Woodwind

HRIS WOOD
DICK HECKSTALL-
SMITH
MIKE VICKERS
Alan Bown
Kenny Ball
Acker Bilke
John Entwhistle
Tubby Hayes
Mike Elliott
Chris Mercer
Klaus Voorman
Alan Skidmore
Ray Davies
Eric Allan Dale
John Anthony
Griff West

1. A
   C
2.
3.

CRIS

CREAM AND HENDRIX TOP POLL

BEAT INSTRUMENTAL

eam

RIX
rs
mend

ichards
/Reid
Nash/Hicks
rd/Blaikley
Mayall
Barrett
Wood

135

136

Brown decried the lack of foresight. "People had absolutely no concept of longevity. Stigwood's initial idea was that Cream were a band who could fill clubs because of their reputations. The first album was like a blues record with a few extra bits. Extremely well played but not terribly well recorded. They were still finding their feet and their musical personalities, and it was actually no indication of what they could do. There was a severe limitation on their work. 'I Feel Free' was also produced by Stigwood, but Jack Bruce began to realise what was going down in the studio and he created something that was so difficult for Stigwood to understand that it was actually hard to fuck up!"

"The basic structure of the thing, which Jack put together, was so good, so resilient and daring, that once you put it in front of a microphone, the thing spoke for itself. That was a real breakthrough and it was probably the only real pop song they ever wrote."

Brown believed Stigwood wanted Cream to be like the Bee Gees; easily manageable pop stars, who would do as they were told. Then the real Bee Gees came along, and the pressure was off Cream.

"Once he let Cream alone, then they could do anything they wanted up to a point. I think he was miffed when Felix came along, because Felix showed him up. The guys didn't want to be produced by Stigwood. They knew there was something more." Brown remembers Ginger Baker actually sabotaging a Stigwood-produced recording session. "He knocked a Coke bottle over and spilt the contents into a recording console which must have cost a few quid. I'm sure it was deliberate. I'm sure they didn't want Stigwood to produce them, although he was a very good manager. He aimed them slightly in the wrong place to start with, but as soon as they started to happen anyway, and break in the States, to his credit, he was able to organise it properly. And he had an enormous eye for talent.

"I think the stuff that Felix Pappalardi produced was faultless. I listen to it now and it still sounds great. He understood perfectly what to do with them. He had real vision. He said: 'I know exactly how to do this band'. He was a superb producer and excellent musician. He persuaded Atlantic to let them into the studio and Stigwood was pissed off because he didn't know much about what was going on. He wasn't aware that something amazing and magical had happened, and only appreciated it when the sales started to happen. Nobody knew how to produce them until Felix came along. He made a fantastic difference."

'Disraeli Gears' was finally released in November 1967, sporting a distinctive day-glo coloured cover designed by Eric's flatmate, the Australian artist Martin Sharp. The album was a brilliant combination of rock, pop and blues that set standards for years to come. It was packed with imaginative songs and performances. The opening cut was 'Strange Brew', a haunting Clapton piece, co-written with Felix Pappalardi and his wife Gail Collins. Several years later, Pappalardi was tragically shot dead by Collins after an argument.

Throughout the album Clapton used considerably more effects than he'd employed on 'Fresh Cream', including a fuzz box and wah wah pedal on his guitar. This suggested he had been spurred on to using a more adventurous sound by Hendrix's example. Most people remember the album for 'Sunshine Of Your Love', the Bruce/Brown collaboration that set the seal on the use of heavy bass riffs in rock. But there were many other fine performances like 'Dance The Night Away', notable for Eric's delicate phrasing, and 'World Of Pain', which Pappalardi apparently wrote about a tree in his garden. On the second side 'Tales Of Brave Ulysses' was another fine Clapton song, co-written with Martin Sharp, and inspired by a visit to the Greek Islands. 'SWLABR' (She Walks Like A Bearded Rainbow) had some typically weird Pete Brown lyrics, including Jack's memorable pronouncement "The rainbow has a beard!".

'We're Going Wrong' was virtually a duet between Baker & Bruce, with Ginger's timpani-style accompaniment gently urging on Jack's poignant vocals. It was one of the most sensitive performances on the album, by two of the band's toughest characters. Eric was much more at home on the funky 'Outside Woman Blues' and played brilliantly on another overlooked Cream concoction 'Take It Back'. This sported clever unison bass and guitar lines, unexpected chord changes and a brisk band performance with minimal freak outs from the rhythm section. The whole piece had a Dylanish-Byrds feel which showed how Cream could have developed along Claptonian lines.

There were two jokey tracks; Ginger's 'Blues Condition' on which he proved he was a much better drummer than a singer, and 'Mother's Lament', a Cockney music hall song, doubtless induced by homesick feelings during their first visit to America. "Shall we do it again?" asks Ginger at the end of the take. Answer came there none.

Chapter Six
GOODBYE CREAM

In the aftermath of their first American trip, Cream faced a dilemma. They had worked hard but didn't seem to be getting any further in the battle for world domination that every band seeks, whether they are Nineties rappers or Sixties rockers. In the first months of 1967, rumours began to spread that the purveyors of the Neasden sound were considering giving it all up. They were still playing small venues at home, and in America they were of minority interest. However, there was too much at stake for the band to break up so soon and even Eric, usually regarded as the most disenchanted Creamite, would describe the mid-period of the band's brief lifespan as its happiest and most rewarding. Certainly there was good news around the corner. 'Strange Brew', accompanied by Clapton's first stab at writing, 'Tales Of Brave Ulysses', was issued as a single in June 1967, and stomped its way up to Number 17 in the UK charts. At the same time 'Fresh Cream' entered the American album charts, helped by their extensive touring. It peaked at Number 39 during a 92 week chart run. It was confirmation that the band could reach a much wider audience. However, Cream's prolific lyricist Pete Brown never went to America with the group.

"I was quite pissed off about that," he says. "The band didn't quite know where I stood, and Stigwood didn't like me very much. I think he regarded me as a necessary evil. The band stuck up for me at various times and said I'd contributed a lot, and I guess he went along with it, but I know he was fairly reluctant."

On July 2 Cream returned to London's Saville Theatre to play a show with the Jeff Beck group and John Mayall's Bluesbreakers. At another Saville show they shared the bill with the Bonzo Dog Doo Dah Band, which proved an hilarious night of madness. The Bonzos threw a dummy out of the Royal Box onto the stage, during a mock altercation, and Eric played with his guitar dangling from chains, his contribution to surreal humour.

In August they headlined on the final day of the seventh annual Jazz & Blues Festival at Windsor, where they'd made their debut the previous year. The same month they began their first proper American tour, with a two week stint at the Fillmore West, San Francisco starting on August 22.

They packed the hall and the fans went mad, much to the band's delight. There wasn't another group in America at that time who could touch them.

Their stage act had expanded to allow time to jam and improvise at length, with such numbers as 'Crossroads', 'Spoonful', 'Traintime' and 'Toad' turning into major epics.

It left critics confused. Some said they were a 'jazz group' while others tried to play down their importance, with slights and snubs. Older American jazz musicians felt threatened by the band's success at playing contemporary improvised music. Drummer Buddy Rich, in particular, vented his spleen against Ginger Baker. Rich was a master drummer, one of the greatest in the world, but in 1967 he was playing old style big band swing and wasn't reaching thousands of young American fans who were making rock music big business.

Rich got his revenge. Playing at the Fairfield Hall, Croydon during a British tour with his big band, he suddenly turned his drum solo into a perfect copy (or parody) of Ginger Baker's solo on 'Toad'. Nobody else in the audience seemed to notice – except me – a fan of both drummers!

The innovations Cream introduced had a more productive effect on younger musicians. Jack Bruce recalls how Steve Swallow, the bass player with Gary Burton, saw the British band at the Fillmore. The next day he went out and bought a bass guitar. "He never played upright again!"

"People like Carla Bley saw the band and so did Miles Davis," says Jack. "We were supposed to play with Miles at a festival in a place called Randall's Island in New York. It was going to be a huge festival with an astounding bill and then the promoter split with the bread and the thing never happened. It was a great pity because it would have been very interesting to play with Miles at that time. He 'went electric' around that time, and I think that was mainly due to the influence of Jimi Hendrix, and to a lesser extent, us too.

"We were sort of like an electric jazz band and we definitely had some influence on him."

HASSLES

The band battled on with its heavy American touring schedule and most of the time got on pretty well together. Says Jack: "There was always a bit of friction between Ginger and myself but mostly we were happy together, especially in the early days and when we went to Europe for the first time. We always hung out together partly out of self preservation. That was because of the way we looked. In those days the public all looked pretty straight, with short hair and suits and ties, but we would be in Afro hair-dos, purple coats and pink boots and God knows what else, and we had to stick together! I remember we were in West Berlin and we wanted to go to East Berlin and check it out. We got as far as Check Point Charlie, saw all the Russian troops, got the horrors and decided not to bother!"

"The middle class American is such a slob – you wouldn't believe it. Life is so comfortable for them, with the car and TV, they don't want to worry and they don't even want to think. It's all very sick."

Jack remembers a more pleasant trip to Belfast in Northern Ireland when they were visited by a 14-year-old guitarist. "That was Gary Moore. He came to see us at the Ulster Hall and he's got some funny stories about Eric – that I can't repeat. He saw a couple of gigs and was very impressed."

Cream played Las Vegas and after the gig returned to their reserved accommodation at the famous Sands hotel.

"The only times I remember getting into real scrapes because of our appearance was in the States. At the Sands they wouldn't let us into our rooms and said that they had overbooked. So we all had to leave. We had to leave Las Vegas as no hotel would have us. You had to be pretty thick-skinned to cope, and it made us very insular. There was a particularly horrendous time in Boston when we were there for a week, at a place called The Psychedelic Supermarket. Boston is very much a red-neck town, although it has this reputation for being civilised. We were really being hassled, so we had to spend all the time we weren't at the gig locked in our hotel room. It was very depressing."

143

Eric Clapton was fascinated by the growing conflict between middle America and the hippies. He gave me his impressions of the changes sweeping the States on his return to London when the psychedelic movement seemed new, exciting and mysterious.

"There is definitely a philosophy of love spreading and it's developing among a wide age group from 15 to 50. It's not so much a reaction against the war as a completely whole new way of life. It's confined to the ghettos of San Francisco and New York, because the middle class in America is still so big. It's not safe to go out of the confines of the ghettos like Greenwich Village. If you are dressed strangely with long hair, reaction against you can be quite frightening. The middle class American is such a slob – you wouldn't believe it. Life is so comfortable for them, with the car and TV, they don't want to worry and they don't even want to think. It's all very sick."

Eric wasn't entirely taken in by the hippy movement either and said perceptively: "The Love Philosophy is a fad in many ways. It involves a new way of dressing and thousands of people are drawn to that, but I don't see much harm in this as long as the people don't prostitute it. There's not so much hate, more apathy. A lot of people seem to get to the point where they are in a dream. They get up, go to work, watch TV and go to bed. What the young people are doing is kick everybody in the stomach and shout 'Look at us – we're having a gas time with people!'"

Eric told how he went to a Be-In in Central Park and saw 20,000 people enjoying themselves. "There were no stages or admission fees. It was a reaction against materialism. I don't know how it was organised. It seemed to spread by word of mouth. At the Be-In there were cops on horses riding round to make sure there was no trouble. After a while the kids started offering the police pop corn and the pop corn was doused in acid. In a couple of hours most of the cops were off their horses walking around in the crowd with hats off and holding flowers in their hands. By sunset they were lying on the grass listening to the drums."

Not all the population were hostile towards the strangely-clad band. They had a particularly warm welcome in Los Angeles. Says Jack: "We were met at the airport by the promoters and record company people and it was really nice. The first time we went to San Francisco we were met by the Hells Angels who brought a psychedelic hearse along. We travelled into town in style with them riding their motorbikes flanking us, with everybody clearing out of the way. The Angels sort of adopted us!"

FLOWER POWER

Although Cream started out as a very British blues band, as the summer of '67 hotted up, they 'went flower power' along with Hendrix, The Stones and even those Geordie stalwarts, The Animals, all of whom sported caftans, beads and bells and wafted incense in their wake.

"Well everybody went psychedelic, didn't they?" laughs Jack. "The Beatles sort of started it all and even The Stones did 'Their Satanic Majesties Request'. Everyone was tripping on acid. But we didn't really get into hard drugs at all in the Sixties. It wasn't until the Seventies that people started to get into the heavier stuff."

The Fillmore Auditorium in San Francisco was a home from home for the British band. It cost a mere three dollars in 1967 to get into the large block building that could house up to 2,000 hippies a night to see such diverse acts as Lightning Hopkins, Country Joe & The Fish and The Yardbirds – a typical bill of the day. When Cream played there, they invariably caused a sensation. The theatre was equipped with nine PA speakers on stage, unheard of in England at that time, and a sophisticated light show which added to the psychedelic, kaleidoscopic effect. At one show (in February 1968) Cream were supported by American Flag. A local critic, one George Almond (a bit of a Cream nut), described the atmosphere in a quaintly-worded contemporary account.

"Spectacular effects were created by a bunch of ardent scraggy technicians huddling over their projectors, swirling coloured wheels, rapid-fire slide magazines and movie projectors. On the screens were movie shorts of a policeman methodically banging his baton against his hand, of preachers smiling sweetly and images of flags, nudes, Nazis and flowers – all constantly changing.
On stage were the stars of the evening, an English group, Cream, which consisted of three musicians of outstanding quality. This we did not know of course when we joined those on the floor who were squatting patiently as the electricians shackled the volume boosters to the Cream's instruments.

The audience hushed in anticipation of deep experience as the Cream trickled on to the stage in bright shirts and piped clashing pants. The gods were there and as the first number exploded into the auditorium it was as though we were witnessing the explosion of a musical megaton bomb. For nearly an hour the message of 1967 roared out.

For many of the Haight Ashbury league this was a musical thrill of rare vintage, whilst for the unenlightened there was a genuine respect for the abilities and talent of the Cream who were undisputed masters of their art. In solos of great length and complexity, the guitar, the mouth organ and the drums were treated to efforts so prodigious that we felt the Cream had gymnastic training for eight hours a day. When at last Cream retired from the stage, there could have been no-one who had not felt some message from a realm beyond normal understanding."

"That was a huge hit and it was the first double album that sold a million and it became a Platinum disc."

Cream had won a great reception on the West Coast, but progress was still slow as far as the rest of the country was concerned. "Our impact on America wasn't as quick as you might expect," says Jack. "We did this very long tour (which began in February 1968), but we didn't get a hit record right away. In fact 'Fresh Cream' didn't really do anything in the States. Then we did 'Disraeli Gears' and that did very well. 'Fresh Cream' became a hit after that."

Their American tour was extended until October and in November 'Disraeli Gears' was released and went to Number Four in the US album chart and charted at Number Five in the UK.

The spectacular, ground-breaking double album, 'Wheels Of Fire' released in August 1968, confirmed the band's status as an international supergroup. Produced by Felix Pappalardi, the first two sides were recorded at the Atlantic Studios in New York. Packaged in distinctive silver covers, the album featured a brilliant new Bruce/Brown song 'White Room', 'Sitting On Top Of The World', 'Passing The Time', 'As You Said', Ginger's peculiar 'Pressed Rat And Warthog', 'Politician', 'Those Were The Days', 'Born Under A Bad Sign' and 'Deserted Cities Of The Heart'.

The second LP comprised live performances recorded at the Fillmore West, San Francisco, with marathon versions of 'Crossroads', 'Spoonful', 'Traintime' and 'Toad'.
The success of 'Wheels Of Fire' made up for all the years of struggle.

"That was a huge hit and it was the first double album that sold a million and it became a Platinum disc," says Jack. "It was presented to us by Ahmet Ertegun and Robert Stigwood at Madison Square Garden at a very strange gig on a revolving stage. It must have been horrible for the audience. They'd get a glimpse of the drums, and then the guitar and then the bass, and then it would all go away and come round again. We did a few bizarre gigs. But we all agreed that the most bizarre one was at Streatham Ice Rink in London where the audience was skating! We also did the Locarno in Glasgow, where I had once worked in the Palais bands. We came round from behind the curtains on a revolving stage to face a very small audience."

It was during their trip to Scotland that the band enjoyed its best times together. They hung out as mates and, as Eric recalls, they were so close they virtually had their own language together that outsiders found difficult to penetrate.

One afternoon, while tripping on acid, they decided to run up and down the slopes of Ben Nevis, the highest mountain in Britain. As Jack remembers, it was easy enough to start running, but virtually impossible to stop. Their assault on the mountain and their collapse, breathless at the bottom, in a way symbolised the career of the band.

RUMOURS

As 1968 dawned more rumours spread that there was unrest in the camp. Ginger Baker, the man who had put the band together, attempted to dispel them with a positive, upbeat mid-term report on the state of Cream.   He assured me: "It's alright most of the time, which is unusual. They put up with me, and I tend to be bad-tempered. It's a progression and it will go on, as we are doing something different all the time. I think it's a load of crap when people say we aren't working out as a group. We have had some plays that have been absolutely tremendous. We draw big crowds and they thoroughly enjoy themselves. We are three totally different personalities and none of us think alike, but we get more and more together musically. It's world class in my opinion and I don't think there are three other musicians about to touch it."

Eric agreed that the band had been very close for a six month

period around the time of 'Disraeli Gears' but heavy touring tended to make life a blur, and as his own musical tastes began to change, he knew he couldn't stay with the band much longer. Some savage criticism in America, when one Rolling Stone writer called him "The master of the blues cliché" was a body blow that convinced him he would have to move on.

The Rolling Stone review was the American rock establishment's revenge. Eric actually fainted when he read it and it hastened the end of the band.

The reasons for the break-up, which came as a great shock to their fans, have been debated over the years, not least by the group themselves.

Ultimately it was the seeds of discontent sown in Eric's heart that made the break-up inevitable. Clapton would sound much more bitter and critical of the band in the immediate aftermath of its demise. Once the harsher memories had faded, he would be able to come back to the subject with pride and even affection.

Although it represented only a relatively short period in a career that has now spanned some thirty years, Cream was a crucial time for Clapton and has never been far from the collective memories of Baker and Bruce.

Jack Bruce agrees that the rot set in quite early on. "A lot of things happened. For a start we got very rich, very quickly, so there wasn't the hunger for success anymore. We had done very well and our lifestyles changed. Suddenly we could buy a couple of houses and a Ferrari or a Bentley. It was very hard to take in. We went from getting two quid for playing the All-Niter at The Flamingo to suddenly getting massive royalties from Platinum album sales. Thinking about it now, it took us years to recover from the Sixties. In fact the next decade was a period of recuperation and re-grouping, although other things happened – like drugs – in the Seventies. You see the Sixties weren't really a period of hard drugs use. There was a bit of dope around but it was a happy, light-hearted time – a wonderful time really. But in the Seventies reality set in."

THE BREAK UP

While it was known as early as May 1968 that the band would break up, official confirmation wasn't given until July when it was announced that the band would make a farewell tour of America. There would be just two concerts in Britain, in November. Cream's British fans were hurt and upset and complaints poured into the music press. It was too late to change their minds.

Pete Brown, still reeling from his own financial success, observed the impending break-up without too much concern. "Artistic satisfaction was more important to them and if they weren't getting it from what they were doing, then it seemed right to break up. We didn't understand commercial considerations in those days," says Brown. "I think the decision to break up was mutual. Musically they had run as far as the limitations of the band would go. I'm sure it was not that much to do with fighting. I never saw any of that. I never saw them being angry with each other. I just saw them being themselves. Sometimes there would be physical explosions, when Jack and Ginger were with Graham Bond. I never saw that around Cream. Eric was always very good-natured. I stayed with him for a while at the Pheasantry in Chelsea until his flat-mate threw me out for being too noisy! I was homeless and Eric got me in there. Eric was very gentle and very nice, but Cream was like being thrown in at the deep end for him. He was a very good, instinctive musician who had studied the blues and R&B, whereas the other two had very powerful jazz and classical credentials, could write and read music well. Eric was more of a player than a writer – and always has been – although he's written well in recent years, now he knows what he wants. He was at a slight disadvantage in Cream, and it must have been hard. And because of that tension existing between the two of them, they would obviously goad Eric. He was capable of being inspired and when you get somebody who is receptive and has a good mind and you put them in an interesting situation, they may rise to it. They may transcend all sorts of limitations they previously thought they had. It's like sex. Some people turn you on, so you perform incredibly, while others just won't and you have to do it yourself! But then you get a situation where if you are not with those people, you might feel quite insecure because it was those people who took you to the heights you reached. Now its kind of frightening, because you can't get back to them. That's maybe what Eric felt."

Brown could see that Baker and Bruce would push him, perhaps further than he sometimes wanted to go.

"He'd do stuff that was very inspired both on record and certainly live. Nobody had played like that before. If you listen to the Grateful Dead, Jerry Garcia would play a thirty minute guitar solo and there would be about three ideas in there. That's alright, because it's like a sort of meditation. But for me, one idea every ten minutes is not enough! Whereas Eric with Cream was happening all the time, and the band were pushing him so it had got to happen. There never was a rhythm section like Baker and Bruce. They were completely inspiring."

Given the pressure on Cream, and Clapton in particular, to perform at full tilt every night, it might have been a good idea to bring in another musician, perhaps Graham Bond to add keyboards. It would have filled out the band's sound, given Eric a rest, and been the making of Bond, who would have relished the chance of playing to huge audiences in America.
Said Pete Brown: "Well we know the reason for that. Stigwood and Graham didn't get on. The band wanted him there. Jack and Ginger loved Graham, despite whatever problems they had with him. They knew he was part of their inspirational make-up. But Stigwood wouldn't entertain it.

To Graham, all management was the enemy anyhow. He was an anarchist! He didn't like authority. It was what the song 'Politician' was all about."

"I think the decision to break up was mutual. Musically they had run as far as the limitations of the band would go. I'm sure it was not that much to do with fighting. I never saw any of that. I never saw them being angry with each other. I just saw them being themselves. Sometimes there would be physical explosions, when Jack and Ginger were with Graham Bond. I never saw that around Cream."

CHANGES

I went to see Eric in the summer at his Chelsea flat and found him perfectly happy and quite excited about the future. He played me tracks by Bob Dylan and The Band and enthused about The Band's own material. "I think this music will influence a lot of people. Everybody I have played it too has flipped," he said. "The band is releasing an album called 'Music From Big Pink' and since I heard all this stuff, all my values have changed. I think it has probably influenced me."

Certainly the new music was more melodic, more laid-back, less frantic and competitive than Cream, and as we smoked some powerful cigarettes, I knew exactly what he meant.

Stumbling to the bus stop in the Kings Road in the early evening sunshine after our interview, I realised that I had witnessed the conversion of Clapton. I had a glimpse of his musical future, that would be revealed in such bands as Blind Faith, Delaney & Bonnie, Derek & The Dominoes, and the many versions of The Eric Clapton Band. He had found a faith that would last a lifetime, and discovered that the blues could be a friend and not an enemy.

You couldn't blame Eric for wanting a change, he had done enough in one particular style, but it still seemed a great shame. Cream contemplated splitting before they had fulfilled their full potential. They could have taken advantage of advances in recording production and better organised stage shows with improved sound and lighting, More sympathetically planned touring schedules would have preyed less on their health and nerves. Crucially, they could have let Eric develop as a writer and singer. These were all factors that would benefit the better-balanced groups that followed them into the Seventies, notably Led Zeppelin. It was even more lamentable that Cream, after their US breakthrough, hardly ever played at home again.

Says Jack Bruce: "We should have played in a lot of places, and of course we should have played large gigs in Britain, and we should have played in Australia and Japan. We only did the States. It was quite a tragedy really. We were asked to play at the Woodstock Festival, but we didn't. A lot of things like that were badly handled."

In May 1968 the band put out 'Anyone For Tennis' a twee Clapton/Sharp composition, coupled with Ginger's 'Pressed Rat And Warthog'. The A-side was written as the theme for a movie called The Savage Seven and featured Eric on acoustic guitar. A promo video was shot of the band dancing around with tennis rackets. It struggled into the charts on the strength of the band's name. The whole aberration could only be put down to the band's celebrated sense of humour. It certainly underlined the strength of the Bruce/Brown writing team, especially when the band's next single, 'Sunshine Of Your Love', became a smash hit. Written by Jack and Pete with assistance from Eric, it was a Top Five hit in America where it sold over a million copies, and reached Number 25 in the UK.

After a three month break, the band bid farewell to America with a tour that began in Oakland, Cal. in the first week of October and ended with a memorable show at Madison Square Garden, New York on November 2 and one last date in Baltimore on November 3. En route they played some 14 American cities, earning 25 thousand dollars a night. At Madison Square Garden, where they received their Platinum disc for 'Wheels Of Fire', they played to 22,000 people.

> *"If I had formed a blues trio, we would have gone on imitating records, as I had been doing with John Mayall. I would never have learned how to play anything of my own. In Cream, I was forced to try and improvise; whether I made a good job of it a lot of the time is debatable."*

Then on November 26 they played two shows to a combined crowd of 10,000 fans at London's Royal Albert Hall. They were supported by Yes, a fine new British band, and Taste, the Irish band led by guitarist Rory Gallagher. Cream's performance was filmed for a BBC TV documentary directed by Tony Palmer, a great fan of the band. The film later became a best-selling video. The reaction at the concert was ecstatic and Cream seemed genuinely surprised.

"I didn't think anyone would remember us," said Eric, fearing they had been away from England for too long.

As the band quit the road, so the final singles and albums came through the pipe line. 'Goodbye' (Polydor) was released in March 1969 and included 'I'm So Glad', 'Politician', 'Sitting On Top Of The World', 'Badge', 'Doing That Scrapyard Thing' and 'What A Bring Down'. It topped the charts in both America and the UK.

Next came 'Live Cream Vol. l' (Polydor) in June 1970 with 'N.S.U.', 'Sleepy Time Time', 'Lawdy Mama', 'Sweet Wine' and 'Rollin' and Tumblin''.

'Live Cream Vol.2' came out in July 1972 featuring 'Deserted Cities Of the Heart', 'White Room', 'Politician', 'Tales Of Brave Ulysses', 'Sunshine Of Your Love' and 'Hideaway'.

'White Room' was released as a single in January 1969, and reached Number Six in the States. It was followed by 'Badge' in April 1969. George Harrison co-wrote 'Badge' with Clapton, and played rhythm guitar on the track under the name of L'Angelo Misterioso. Eric often guested with his heavy friends, and played on Harrison's 'While My Guitar Gently Weeps' on The Beatles 'White Album'.

In 1994, more 'fresh' Cream material was found in the vaults for a projected third volume of 'live' performances from their American tour.

JNNER MOUNTJNG FLAMES

In the years after Cream's demise, Clapton revealed his inner frustrations with the concept of the band and repeated that he originally thought it was going to be a simple blues trio. "We were going to play small clubs... we didn't want to be big in any way. We had gigs when you could have mistaken us for Hendrix, it was so good... but on a bad night.."

Eric also bared his feelings about his cohorts: "Those guys were pretty strong personalities. I hadn't taken that into consideration. At the first rehearsal, most of my ambition to lead the group went out of the window, because I realised I didn't have the wherewithal. When it came to forceful personalities, Ginger was the man, and Jack was vying for the role."

"So I just let them get on with it, and backed off. There was a constant battle between Ginger and Jack. They loved each others' playing but they couldn't stand the sight of each other. I was the mediator and I was getting tired of that. Then Rolling Stone called me the 'master of the blues cliché' which just about knocked me cold. At that time I decided I was going to leave Cream."

But in an interview with Robert Palmer in Rolling Stone in 1988, Eric confirmed that in the long term, Cream had been a worthwhile, important experience for him: "If I had formed a blues trio, we would have gone on imitating records, as I had been doing with John Mayall. I would never have learned how to play anything of my own. In Cream, I was forced to try and improvise; whether I made a good job of it a lot of the time is debatable."

The nature of the band and its heavy reliance on improvisation during long concerts, meant that naturally there were moments when they weren't inspired. Some felt that Cream's jamming went on too long and was prone to fall back on stock phrases. It was the same criticism that could be directed at pure jazz groups, (and had been for years by previous generations of critics). Jack Bruce doesn't agree with such criticism.

"I honestly don't think that's fair. A lot of the time when we were jamming it was completely magical. I just remember it as being very intense. We even had a thing with Eric when he'd play an unaccompanied solo, and that was great. It never went beyond the point of no return. I never found it that way. Ginger's drum solos were often very long, but they developed a form and told a story. Maybe some people didn't like it. If they can't take a couple of choruses of the blues, what do they want? I think people like to hear a bit of playing. I remember going to hear Duke Elllington's Orchestra and hearing their tenor sax player Paul Gonsalves playing chorus after chorus on 'Diminuendo And Crescendo In Blue' which was a very fast blues, and I didn't want it to stop! Some people say that's being 'self indulgent', but I say it's being creative. I just love improvised music. For some people, one chorus can be too long."

Whatever the causes and circumstances of the break-up, and despite the criticisms of their alleged musical excesses, in retrospect the band feel it was all done from the best motives. "We did Cream in a very idealistic way," says Jack Bruce. "There wasn't any great master plan. It was just a question of doing what we believed in. The more attention the band gets now, the happier I am because I tend to think Cream has got a bit overlooked in recent years."

"Led Zeppelin was obviously a much more commercially successful band and lasted much longer, but it came in after Cream and Jimi Hendrix created this vast so-called 'underground' audience for rock, which was actually bigger than anything else. I'm not knocking Zeppelin but they took advantage of the huge vacuum left by us, Hendrix and The Beatles who all finished around the same time. There were no more big bands left by the end of the Sixties. The whole heavy rock thing really started with Cream and that should be remembered. It was an important band."

"I think it would be nice to recreate Cream one day. Although everybody said the album we did with Gary Moore sounded liked Cream, for a start it had a keyboard player on more than half of the songs. My point is that myself and Ginger Baker pre-date Cream for yonks. We were playing together for five years as a rhythm section in a lot of different situations. Obviously I love Eric's playing very much and would like to play with him again."

The band said their goodbyes on friendly terms and, says Jack: "Immediately afterwards it was quite good actually. I remember Eric coming round to my house in London and hanging out. I remember going to see Ginger's band Airforce when they played at The Albert Hall. It was great because it was like a big weight off of us. Cream had been such an intense period of activity. What we should have done, and what I suggested at the time, was that we should split up, but that we should come together occasionally to make a record or do a concert. But that didn't work out for whatever reason. At that point Eric had become quite ambitious and set out on the road to become a star. But there were no bad feelings about Cream. We just got involved in our own things and grew apart really. A lot of things were said by each of us in interviews later that maybe upset each other."

163

"We weren't together anymore and may have said some things that caused bad feelings which grew out of all proportion. Then, of course, we did finally get together again in 1993 at the Rock'N'Roll Hall Of Fame. We played three songs and hung out for a couple of days and as far as I was concerned there was no more bad feeling. I play with Ginger again for God's sake – and we get on really well!"

In 1994 Ginger and Jack teamed up with the guitar player who had gone to see Cream play in Belfast as a teenager back in the Sixties. Gary Moore played the lead guitar in Baker, Bruce & Moore and the spirit of Cream wasn't far absent from the exciting music they made together on tour and on a well-received album. As Gary played so well, some felt that there was no longer any pressing need to recreate the original Cream, in the way that fans constantly yearned for a Led Zeppelin reunion. But Jack Bruce in the summer of 1994 didn't see it that way.

"I think it would be nice to recreate Cream one day. Although everybody said the album we did with Gary Moore sounded liked Cream, for a start it had a keyboard player on more than half of the songs. My point is that myself and Ginger Baker pre-date Cream for yonks. We were playing together for five years as a rhythm section in a lot of different situations. Obviously I love Eric's playing very much and would like to play with him again."

"As a rhythm section we made him go for it in those Cream days and he certainly took more risks and achieved a lot. Even at the Rock'N'Roll Hall Of Fame, which was a kind of strange gig, he really played well. It was filmed and the video will end up in a museum. Peace at last! But I don't shut the door on a Cream reunion again. It would be great to do a charity concert because the band has a magic name. I wouldn't be happy to go out on the road though. I had very mixed feelings when a lot of offers came up. It would be going back in a way, whereas with Gary Moore we were going forward. Cream is something that happened in the Sixties, and it was great, and it would be so difficult to achieve as much now. It would be nice to re-record some of our greatest hits. I wouldn't mind doing 'I Feel Free' on 48- tracks! I like David Bowie's version on his last album and there's a hip-hop version of 'Sunshine Of Your Love' by George Clinton. It would be nice for us to do something like that!"

Cream sold some 35 million albums during its life span and the records have gone on selling, to become part of the heritage of rock music. Some 26 years later, they still sound fresh, original and exciting. Their music was created as a result of the passions and obsessions of youth, during an extraordinary period of great social upheaval. Such times and such music can never be repeated.

AFTERMATH

It seemed a kind of folly to reintroduce another supergroup, just when Eric Clapton had recovered from the traumas of Cream. Yet the next step for the Robert Stigwood Organisation was to launch Eric with a new band called Blind Faith. The line-up included Ginger Baker, back on drums, Steve Winwood on vocals and keyboards, and Rick Grech on bass. Although Eric had always wanted to team up with Steve Winwood, the teenaged musical prodigy from the Spencer Davis Group and Traffic, the new band proved to be a disappointment.

They produced one excellent album in 1969, but from their first appearance at a free concert in Hyde Park in June, 1969, it seemed as if the band was too laid-back and unsure of itself. Apparently they had been smoking heavily behind the amplifiers before they went on, to calm their nerves. They played the Buddy Holly song 'Well Alright', 'I'd Rather See You Sleeping On The Ground', 'Sea Of Joy', 'Means To An End' and the Stones' 'Under My Thumb'. Even the best efforts of Ginger Baker failed to spark some life into the outfit.

The band went to Scandinavia and then to America for a tour that drew big crowds and earned them a lot of money. The US tour opened at the Newport Jazz Festival on July 11, 1969. But Eric quickly grew tired of all the hype and over-heated expectations of a thrill hungry audience and realised he was back on the old Cream style treadmill. He met and became friendly with Delaney & Bonnie, their support group, and carried on touring with them when the Blind Faith dates finished. In January 1970 Blind Faith split up and Eric teamed up with Delaney & Bonnie & Friends for a US tour that included Dave Mason and George Harrison. In March he recorded his first solo album 'Eric Clapton'. Clapton was encouraged to develop his talents as a singer and writer by Delaney Bramlett, but when the latter bust up with his band, Eric took it over to form what became known as Derek & The Dominoes. The anonymity was an attempt to hide away from the burden of Eric's 'guitar hero' image, and succeeded – too well!

They recorded the classic album 'Layla and Other Assorted Love Songs', but the public were confused and failed to recognise its worth. When the record was a flop, Eric retreated into drug addiction and later drink problems blighted his life during the early Seventies.

167

Respected author Harry Shapiro, who has written books on Jimi Hendrix and Eric Clapton, including Lost In The Blues, was a Cream fan who queued for hours to see the band play at The Marquee Club during their heyday. He has his own theories about the causes of the break-up and the reasons for Clapton's subsequent descent into drug abuse.

"They did get into a rut and they were fed up with playing the same numbers night after night, and the old animosities between Jack and Ginger that had been buried to get the band off the ground, began to surface. They were all staying in separate hotels and travelling separately to gigs by the end. You can't maintain a working situation with that going on. Eric was fed up with being the fastest gun in the west. It made Blind Faith a bit of an irony, because it would be even worse than Cream in that respect."

Shapiro recalls that there were people actually fighting at their concerts in America. When the band played at the Los Angeles on August 15, the house lights were turned on while police chased members of the audience, many of whom were intent on turning the supergroup show into a riot.

"The band was doomed from the start." says Shapiro. "Eric was only in his mid-twenties when all the adulation was going on and we can only imagine what it was like. In those days the pressure was on to deliver all the time. Nowadays, a performer like Sting will only do an album every two years. He gets his Grammy awards and the album sells in trillions. Nobody turns round to Sting and says 'Don't leave it too long mate, or they'll all have forgotten about you'. But then not doing anything for two years was unheard of. I always thought that Eric used drugs as a kind of excuse. He had a medical reason to shut the door and walk away. I don't think it was a conscious decision, but it was convenient in that sense. Of course he then got into booze which had a much bigger chance of finishing him off than the drugs did. He really didn't get it together properly until the early-Eighties. It took him a long time. Unfortunately poor old Jimi Hendrix didn't have a chance to re-invent himself. He too would have stepped back from a career that was becoming a dead end. It is exhausting for an artist when he wants to do something new and everybody rejects it.

Record companies and audiences conspire against you. When they go to a concert they want to hear the hits, not some new piece you've just worked out. When Eric played a night of all blues at the Royal Albert Hall in 1993 somebody yelled out for 'Layla' and he just said: 'Next year'."

'Layla' (co-written with Eric's drummer Jim Gordon), eventually became a hit and virtually become Eric's anthem. By the Eighties Eric had put all his past problems behind him and he became a mature, respected and much-loved performer, leading a succession of excellent bands and always ready to sit in with friends, from George Harrison to Bob Dylan. In 1987 he began the first of his celebrated series of annual seasons at London's Royal Albert Hall, during which he put together one of his finest bands, with Phil Collins on drums. He revamped 'Layla', breathing new life into the old song with his gentle new reggae-tinged version recorded for MTV's celebrated Unplugged.

His life, full of tragedies and triumphs, has seen him elevated to the role of an international celebrity status that has gone far beyond anything imagined even at the height of his fame in the Sixties.

> *"Eric was fed up with being the fastest gun in the west. It made Blind Faith a bit of an irony, because it would be even worse than Cream in that respect."*

Cream's drummer, meanwhile, with typical energy and enthusiasm created his own dream band, Ginger Baker's Airforce, which featured many musicians he most admired, including Graham Bond, Phil Seamen, Denny Laine and Steve Winwood. Alas, the high flying band lost money and the subsequent tax problems meant that Ginger had to live abroad for many years.

In between playing with the Baker Gurvitz Army, and more recent Masters Of Reality, Ginger embarked on many adventures, from driving across the Sahara desert to running a recording studio in Africa, and from playing polo to growing olives in Italy. He now lives in America and was recently reunited with Jack Bruce in BBM – Baker, Bruce and Moore.

Says Ginger: "I did the record 'Around The Next Dream' (Virgin) with Gary Moore and Jack and Tommy Ayre on keyboards. Gary and Jack both sang and some of it sounds like Cream. It was pretty frightening! Gary was great to work with. It was real cool, real natural. I got on with Jack really well and it's been pleasurable working with him again. I'm surprised to say that. He's mellowed out a bit. The album went very well and we had a great time."

171

Blind Faith, Hyde Park, June 1969.

Jack enjoyed a busy and varied solo career after Cream, recording a succession of albums and working with American jazz drummer Tony Williams in the band Lifetime. He also worked with guitarist Leslie West, in West, Bruce and Laing, and collaborated with Carla Bley, Larry Coryell, Robin Trower, Mick Taylor and Charlie Watts.

He became involved in world music and classical music and toured Europe with a 13 piece fusion orchestra. During 1992 he toured with a powerhouse trio featuring American guitarist Blues Saraceno and drummer Simon Phillips. Then in 1994 he helped form BBM which played successful shows in Britain, including a secret show at London's Marquee and a sell-out concert at the Brixton Academy on June 5.

"I did the record with Gary Moore and Jack and Tommy Ayre on keyboards. Gary and Jack both sang and some of it sounds like Cream. It was pretty frightening!"

While Clapton's career nose-dived in the early-Seventies and then soared to spectacular heights, Baker and Bruce never managed to achieve the same kind of success or acclaim they had enjoyed in Cream. Indeed, they went through some hard financial times, and there were disputes over royalty payments that were not resolved until the early-Nineties. It transpired that Cream were on a three per cent royalty, which meant they got one per cent each, and for some years Jack Bruce didn't get any royalties at all.

"In Cream we were getting something like one per cent royalty on record sales, between us, explains Ginger. "We were actually each getting less than one per cent. The record company took the major share. Our label was RSO Records which was also our management. Stigwood sold it all to Polygram and they've been taking management commission since that day which was not really on, since they weren't doing any management. But they've back dated that now."

Now that the bad memories have faded, Cream has slipped into perspective for its fans as well as its ex-members. Says Jack Bruce: "I saw an old video of us playing 'Crossroads' in the Sixties that was just steaming – it was outrageous. That was a good band and perhaps more special than any band I've been in. It's funny, I remember when we first rehearsed and did 'I Feel Free' I said: 'Ginger, you gotta go bomp, bomp, bomp on the drums'. He said: 'You're mad!' It started on the wrong beat, with an acapella vocal. We had some terrible fights about that. But they got used to it! The trouble we had was with the record company. They couldn't understand our songs like 'White Room' at all. Yes, there was a competitive thing in Cream, but I liked that. Bands can be too respectful sometimes!"

When Cream played their reunion set at the Rock'N'Roll Hall Of Fame Awards, at the Central Plaza Hotel, Los Angeles, on January 12, 1993, fans paid up to $1,000 a ticket to see what was their first official gig since the farewell show at the Royal Albert Hall in 1968.

It was an emotional moment to see Eric back on guitar, with Jack on bass and vocals and Ginger pounding his drums. They tore through 'Sunshine Of Your Love', 'Crossroads' and 'Born Under A Bad Sign' with all their old fire.

Afterwards Eric said simply: "I was reunited with two people I love very dearly. It was very moving."